URDHVAG AMLAPITTA

Hetu & Nidanparivarjan

AUTHOR NAME

DR PARAG VISHWAS KULKARNI

READER & HOD ROGNIDAN EVAM VIKRITI VIGYAN DEPT.

DR DEEPAK PATIL AYURVEDIC MEDICAL COLLEGE & RESEARCH CENTER BORPADLE KOLHAPUR

DR AMAR BALIRAM ABHRANGE

READER & HOD KRIYA SHARIR DEPT.

DR DEEPAK PATIL AYURVEDIC MEDICAL COLLEGE & RESEARCH CENTER BORPADLE KOLHAPUR

2024

LORD DHANWANTARI

From the Desk of the Authors

In the contemporary world, the dynamics of health and disease have undergone significant transformations. Our lifestyles have evolved with rapid technological advancements, altering our dietary habits, stress levels, and overall health paradigms. One notable consequence of these changes is the increased prevalence of digestive disorders, particularly Urdhvag Amlapitta, commonly known as Hyperacidity or GERD.

The concept of Urdhvag Amlapitta, as delineated in classical Ayurvedic texts, provides a comprehensive understanding of the pathogenesis, etiology, and management of this condition. Despite the profound insights offered by Ayurveda, there exists a gap in the application of these ancient principles to address the contemporary manifestations of this disorder. This book, "URDHVAG AMLAPITTA - HETU & NIDAN PARIVARJAN," aims to bridge this gap by integrating classical wisdom with modern clinical practices.

The need for this book in the current scenario is paramount. The escalating incidence of Urdhvag Amlapitta can be attributed to multiple factors, including erratic dietary habits, increased consumption of processed and fast foods, chronic stress, and sedentary lifestyles. These factors collectively contribute to the imbalance of doshas, particularly Pitta, leading to the manifestation of acid reflux. Conventional treatments often focus on symptomatic relief rather than addressing the root cause of the disorder. This approach may offer temporary respite but fails to provide a long-term solution.

"URDHVAG AMLAPITTA - HETU & NIDAN PARIVARJAN" emphasizes the importance of identifying and eliminating the root causes (Hetu) and modifying lifestyle and dietary practices (Nidan Parivarjan) to achieve holistic health. By adopting a comprehensive approach that includes dietary recommendations, lifestyle modifications, and Ayurvedic therapeutic interventions, this book aims to offer a sustainable solution for managing Urdhvag Amlapitta.

We have meticulously compiled this book to serve as a valuable resource for practitioners, students, and individuals seeking to understand and manage Urdhvag Amlapitta effectively. Our endeavor is to empower readers with the knowledge and tools necessary to address this condition from its roots, thereby promoting overall well-being.

In presenting this book, we acknowledge the timeless wisdom of Ayurveda and its relevance in addressing modern health challenges. We hope that "URDHVAG AMLAPITTA - HETU & NIDAN PARIVARJAN" will contribute to the betterment of health and the alleviation of suffering caused by digestive disorders.

We express our gratitude to the scholars, practitioners, patients and our family members who have inspired and supported us in this endeavor. May this book serve as a beacon of knowledge and a guide to holistic health.

Dr. Parag Vishwas Kulkarni. MD (Rognidan Evam Vikriti Vigyan)
Dr. Amar Baliram Abhrange. MD (Kriya Sharir)

INDEX

1. <u>Introduction:</u>

स्वस्थस्य स्वास्थ्यरक्षणमं आतुरस्य व्याधिपरिमोक्षः ।

In the pursuit of perfect cure, mankind has evolved various system of medicine. Amongst these systems, "*Ayurved* – the science of life" is the most indigenous system of medicine which has propagated treatment of various illnesses.

The main aim of *Ayurved* is to maintain the health of the healthy person and to cure the illness of the diseased person. It is capable of dealing with problems related with modern life-style.

Present book uncovers one of such burning problems i.e. '*Urdhvag AmplaPitta*'. When a casual survey is taken, it is observed that about 60-70% of the patients visiting to OPD's are suffering from this disorder with various intensities, which ultimately disturbs the health and happiness of the individuals.

This book is mainly concentrated on certain prominent '*Hetu*' which are described in our *Ayurvedic* texts under various categories like *Aaharaj Hetu, Viharaj Hetu, Manasik Hetu* etc. Moreover nowadays people do not follow the rules like '*Dincharya*' and '*Rutucharya*'. All these things disturb the balance of '*Tridosha*'.

All the above factors disturb the '*Pitta*' Dosha. In *Amlapitta* there is mainly vitiation of *Pitta Dosha*. Normally *Pitta* has *Katu rasa* but when *Katu Rasa* is converted into *Amla Rasa*, it is called vitiation of *Pitta Dosha*. Vitiated *Pitta* creates several diseases, *Amlapitta* is one of them.

Amlapitta was first mentioned clearly in *Kashyapa Samhita. MadhavaNidana, Bhavaprakasha* and *Yoga Ratnakara* have also described it very well.

Acharya Kashyapa and *Madhavakara* have mentioned psychological problems and bad food habits as the causative factors of *Amlapitta. Acharya Charaka* said that the *Ama* or undigested food molecules which are generated from *Ajirna* are absorbed and deposited in different organs of the body and thus produces the metabolic disease like *Amlapitta*.

It will be helpful for us to avoid such kind of *Hetu* (i.e. *Nidan-parivarjan*) and remain safe, unaffected from such a serious problem.

संक्षेपतः क्रियायोगो निदानपरिवर्जनम्।। - (सु.उ. १/२५)

Sushruta has given importance to *Nidan Parivarjan*. While explaining he defines *Nidan Parivarjan* as to leave or to avoid the causative factors. *Sushruta* further said that *Nidan Parivarjan* should be the first line action against disease.

It includes all type of *Hetu*, i.e. *Dosha Karak Hetu* and *Roga Karak Hetu*, all types of *Hetu* which can be avoided are considered for *Nidan Parivarjan*.

According to *Charaka* although treatment in the form of medicine is mentioned, *Nidan Parivarjan* with that medicine is beneficial for getting total relief i.e. *Apunarbhav Chikitsa*. *Nidan Parivarjan* destroys disease from its root; hence chances of recurrence are less.

संशोधनं संशमनं निदानस्य च वर्जनम् ।
एतावद भिषजा कार्ये रोगे रोगे यथाविधि ।। - (च.वि.)

Sanshodhana, Shaman etc. kriya are of no use if *Nidan Parivarjan* is not achieved. Hence *Nidan Parivarjan* has given place, prior to *Sanshodhan* and *Shaman*.

In other words, if *Nidan Parivarjan* is achieved; then probability of getting disease is much more less than other.

In addition *Nidan Parivarjan* gives a break through in *Samprapti*. If there will be no *Samprapti Vighatan*, then that disease will not be cured totally.

Hence, an attempt is made in this book to understand these *Hetu & Nidan Parivarjan* of *Urdhvag Amlapitta*.

2. <u>Aims and Objectives:</u>

1. To study the *'Hetu'* of *Urdhvag Amlapitta* described in *Ayurvedic* classics.

2. To assess the importance of *Nidan Parivarjan* along with administration of *Guduchi Satva.*

3. To observe the role of these *'Hetu'* in the *Anshansha Samprapti* of the disease on the basis of signs and symptoms occurred.

4. To study some other *'Hetu'* of the disease which are routinely found in this modern era and co-relate them with *Ayurvedic* classics.

5. To observe the prevalence of the disease in various *Prakruti.*

3. <u>Review of Literature:</u>

3.1 <u>Conceptual Study:</u>

Brief Review of *Annavah Srotas:*

***Rachanatmak & Kriyatmak* Aspect:**

- ***Nirukti :-***

The word *Annavaha Srotasa* means the channel through which food is transported. The functions of organs of *ANNAVAHA SROTAS* (Alimentary system) concerned with *ANNA AADANA* (ingestion of food), *ANNA PACHANA* (digestion), *SARA KITTA VIVECHANA* (Separation of nutrient and waste portions) and *RASA SHOSHANA* (Absorption of nutrients)

- ***Moola:-***

➢ According to *Charaka - Amashaya & Vamparshva*

➢ According to *Sushruta - Amashaya & Annavahi Dhamanya.*

Charaka has said that *Amashaya* and *Vamparshva* are the *Moola* of *Annavaha Srotasa.* *Acharya Sushruta* has said that *Amashaya* and *Annavahi Dhamanya* are the *Moola* of *Annavaha Srotasa.*

Chakapani has given two terminologies - *Urdhva* and *Adho* for *Amashya.* *Urdhva Amashaya* is the place of *kapha* while *Adho Amashaya* is the place of *Pitta.*

The deglutination and ingestion process of food is start from mouth and in upper part of the stomach. Main digestive process starts from stomach. Digestive juices secret from lower part of the stomach and intestine. Bile and pancreatic juices secret from liver and pancreas then after come into the small intestine.

Therefore we can include oesophagus and upper part of the stomach in *Urdhva Amashaya* and lower part of the stomach & small intestine in *Adho Amashaya.*

The *Annavahi Dhamanyas* are also the *Moola* of *Annavaha Srotasa.* It means the channels which transport the end products of Anna from the intestine to the plasma blood. Under the microscope the mucous membrane of the small intestine contains millions of finger like projections known as villa. This villa is lined by a single layer of epithelial cells and small arteries, veins and lymphatic vessels. In function, the villa act as a semi permeable membrane and permit the passage of digested food through the *Rasavaha* and *Raktavaha Srotas* present in them. In other words, these microscopic parts of the membrane carry out the transportation of the *Anna Rasa* though the intestinal barrier.

- ***Pittadhara Kala :-***

Acharya Sushruta & Vagbhatta both have described *Pittadhara Kala. Acharya Sushruta* says, The sixth *Kala* situated between *Pakvashaya* and *Amashaya* is the *Pittadhara Kala* and it is known as *Grahani.* In his view, the integrity of *Grahani* depends upon Agni. In *charak's* opinion *Grahani* is so called because it receives and retains the food for the duration of its digestion. He observed that the food, which has reached the *Amashaya* after under going digestion, is absorbed.

Pittadhara Kala provides the digestive juices collectively termed as *Pachakagni* or *Jatharagni.* These juices not only digest the food but also aid the separation of the *Sara* from the *Kittabhaga. (Sara Kitta Vibhajana Kriya)*

The description of *Pittadhara Kala* shows that it is a macroscopic structure which not only serves as a protective lining of the small intestine membrane, but also as a secreting and absorbing structure.

- ***Samana Vayu :-***

Vagbhatta said that *Samana Vayu* is present near the *Agni* and responsible for the reception, digestion, separation and propulsion of the food. The *Samana Vayu* functions are similar to intrinsic nervous system of the stomach and intestine. This system is related to brain and spinal cord. The peristaltic movements of intestine are responsible for mechanically breakdown of intestinal contents and thoroughly mixing up with the juice of pancreas, liver and intestine. They absorbed through the intestinal wall. This has been described the function of *Samana Vayu* as digestion of food, separation of nutrient fractions of food and expulsion of undigested food. *(Annapachana, Vivechana and Munchana.)*

So, as an anatomical view, we can consider fallowing organs & systems in *annavaha Srotasa.*

(A*) Amashaya :-*

(i) *Urdhava* :- (a) Oesophagus

       (b) Upper part of the stomach

(ii) *Adho* : -   (a) Lower part of the stomach

       (b) Small intestine

(B*) Pittadhara Kala:-*

Inner layer of mucous membrane of the small intestine and lower part of the stomach.

(C) *Annavahi Dhamanya:-*

The channels that receive the end particles of the food from the intestine.

(D*) Samana Vayu:-*

Intrinsic nervous system of the stomach & small intestine.

3.2) Pathophysiology:

Shad Ahara Parinamakara Bhava are responsible for proper digestion. (*Ch. Su.* 6/14)

- ### *Ushma:*

Ushma is a quality of *Agni Mahabhuta*. In this regard two terms are to be considered viz. *Agni* and *Pitta*. *Sushruta* explains that there is no *Agni* except *Pitta* in body. *Pachaka Pitta* is situated in *Aamashaya* and it performs the function of *Agni*. Various secretion of G.I.T. can be considered under the light of *Pachaka-Pitta*. It should be released in proper time and in proper quantity. *Ushma* of *Pachaka Pitta* is essential for proper digestion; disturbance of it will lead to complication of *Agni*.

- ### *Vayu:*

Samana Vayu is seated in *Aamashaya,* helps the *Pachaka Pitta* in digestion. According to *Sushruta,* there is a vicious cycle between *Prana-Apana-Samana,* it means this two also helps to maintain *Agni.* Three phases of gastric acid secretion can be considered under the *Karma* of *Vayu.* Phases are as follows –

➢ Cephalic phase

➢ Gastric phase

➢ Intestinal phase

The *Apakarshana, Grahana* and *Munchana Karma* of *Vayu* are essential for proper digestion.

Any exacerbation or cessation in these function will leads to improper digestion. As certain time is required for proper digestion, delayed emptying will cause the *Shuktapaka* and formation of *Ama Visha,* which are the essential factors of *Grahani Dosha.* Now it is clear that all secretary regulations can be termed as function of *Samana Vayu.* If *Samana Vayu* is disturbed it will lead to *Ajirna* stage like and start the pathogenesis of G.I.T. diseases. The etiological factors like *Krodha, Shoka, Bhaya, Chinta* and other stress factors work through the Vagus chain, which is said to be mediating through *Vayu.* Provocation of *Vata* by any factor will result in hyper-secretions leading to hyperacidity.

- ### *Kleda:*

This factor is necessary for proper digestion; it loosens and emulsifies the food. This function is performed mainly by liquid portion of food itself i.e. saliva, mucosa and liquid portion of various digestive juices.

Kledaka and *Bodhaka Kapha* may be considered in this regard. *Drava* has been termed as *Kleda* in *Ahara Parinamakar Bhava.*

Though *Kapha* has not been mentioned having *Drava* quality, but *Kapha* made up of *Apa Dhatu* and so that *Kapha* must posses *Dravata,* but it depends upon the temperature. So, the function of *Kledaka*

Kapha can be summarized as *Kledana-Shithilikaran-Mrudukarana* and *Sanghata Bheda*. The excessive *Klinnata* may hamper the *Agni* directly as mentioned in the literature, that *Dravata* ceases the *Agni*. Ingestion of any *Ati-Ushna*, *Tikshna* and *Katu Dravya* may cause excessive secretion of mucous, which may interfere with digestion process and cause the *Vidagdha Avastha* in excess leading to *Ajirna* etc. In the same way increase in *Kapha* causes *Mandagni*.

- ### *Sneha:*

Usually *Ahara* contains *Sneha*. *Kapha* is also having the property of *Sneha*, it also belongs to *Apa Mahabhuta*. *Sneha* has been described possessing a specific quality of *Apa*. *Pitta* is also having *Sneha Guna* (*Ch. Su.* 7/60). Hence, it can be said that, *Sneha* is also the quality of *Kledaka Kapha* and *Pachaka Pitta* mainly of saliva and glycoprotein of stomach as indigenous *Sneha* and other *Sneha* coming from *Ahara*, Sneha perform the function of *Mardava* (softness of food stuff). Ultimately it helps in the proper mastication and churning by stomach musculature, so that the proper digestion can take place. The decrease in the quality of *Sneha* may damage the intestinal mucosa due to roughness of food stuff and also due to *Ruksha Guna* of various food materials. Decrease of *Sneha* in stomach will lead to provocation of *Samana Vayu* which imbalances the *Agni*.

- ### *Kala:*

This is an important factor for every process to carry out. Time required for the proper secretion of all the digestive factors and for digestion and absorption. Kala means mainly the time required for the digestion of ingested food stuff. But other time considerations are also necessary for proper digestion and absorption of food, i.e. *Kshudha Kala*, *Trushna Kala*, *Dosha Kala* and also *Charvan Kala*. The food is to be taken after the proper digestion of pervious meal. The meal taken without proper digestion of previous meals is called as *Adhyashana* and this is the main cause of *Agnidushti*.

Emptying of stomach requires certain time. Retention of food material in intestine is regulated by *Vayu*. Any disturbance of *Vata* will disturb the *Grahana* and *Munchana* period leading to improper digestion and absorption which will lead to further provocation of *Doshas*. Excessive *Dharana* of acidified *Anna* may cause damage to duodenal mucosa. The A*dhyashana* and *Ajirna-Bhojana*, may cause the *Prakopa* of all the three *Doshas,* simultaneously *Agnidushti*.

- ### *Samayoga:*

Equilibrium of all above factors is necessary for the proper digestion of ingested food material. *Ashtavidha Aahara Aayatana* should be considered to avoid *Agnidushti. Charaka* has given a deep thinking on various aspects of qualities of food materials, which is obvious from the fact that most of the diseases have a long list of etiological factors from dietary habits and diet articles. *Charaka* has formulated guidelines for a healthy diet selection and same time he has also formulated the rules for healthy eating. (*Ch. Vi.* 1/21-22)

<u>3.3) *Ahar Paka Kriya:-*</u>

The *Ahara* undergoes two processes for complete digestion.

(A) *Avasthapaka*

(B) *Vipaka*

In *Ayurved,* the digestion and metabolism is related to *Agni.*

Mainly the *Pachaka Pitta* is responsible for the digestion of food.

The *Pachaka Pitta* is situated in *Grahani* that directly participates in the digestion of food. *Grahani* is also considered as a *Pittadhara Kala.*

Avastha Paka *is the first phase and *Vipaka* is the second phase. *Avasthapaka* is the first phase of the digestion completed by *Pachakagni* in *Annavaha Srotasa*, and *Vipaka* is the second phase of digestion that completed by *Bhutagni* and *Dhatvagni. Vipaka* starts after *Avasthapaka.*

<u>(A) *Avasthapak:-*</u>

There are three stages of *Avasthapaka-*

(i) *Madhur Avasthapaka*

(ii) *Amla Avasthapaka*

(iii) *Katu Avasthapaka*

(i) Madhura Avasthapaka:-

Four type of *Ahara dravyas* like *Asita, Pita, Lidha* and *Khadita* that reaches to *Amashaya* forms in to *Madura Bhava.* At this stage salivary digestion will be completed in the fundus of stomach, where the insoluble starch and polysaccharides converted in to soluble dextrin under the influence of salivary amylase. The final Rasa in the upper portion of the *Urdhava Amashaya* is *Madhura.*

The *Prana Vayu* is responsible for the entire movement of food from the mouth to *Amashaya.* The *Bodhaka Kapha* and *Kledaka Kapha* are also responsible for *Madhura Avasthapaka. Bodhaka Kapha* is responsible for perception of taste in the mouth. The *Bodhaka Kapha* is analogue of saliva which dissolves some substances, the enzyme content begins to act and it lubricates the food, *Kledaka Kapha* also lubricates the food in *Amashaya.* We can consider it as mucine.

(ii) Amla Avasthapaka:-

An *Amla* type of strava occurs here, and after completion of it Ahara becomes *Amla.* So it is called *Amla Avasthapaka.*

In this stage *Ahara* converted in to insoluble proteins to soluble proteins, under the influence of the pepsin, in the presence of HCl. According to *Charaka* and *Vagbhata* the final out come of the entire gastric digestion is the acidified chime, that is interpreted by ' *Tikakar Chakapani* as *Pakva-Apakva* (partially digested). At this phase the *Ahara Pachana* is due to an *Amla* factor secreted by the *Urdhva Amashaya.* The *Ahara* which becomes *Amla Bhava*, passes in to the next lower portion of *Annavaha Srotasa*, were *Achha Pitta* is secreted.

Modern science says that the acidified chime passes down from the pylorus in to the duodenum, stimulates the duodenal glands (Burner's gland) to secrete a number of internal secretion like secretin, cholecystokinin, enterogastrone, Pancreozymine etc. Presences of acid in duodenum liberate the circulation of secretin hormone and stimulate the flow of pancreatic juice. Secretin also enhances the secretion of bile and intestinal juice.

The pancreozymine and intestinal hormone also stimulates the secretions of enzymes from the pancreas, it occurs in intestinal mucosa. Cholecystokinin is also responsible for the contraction of the gall bladder and therefore discharges of bile in duodenum. All these hormones acts due to entering the acidified chime in to duodenum and there fore pancreatic juices, bile and intestinal juices are secreted in small intestine.

In *Ayarved, Achha Pitta* is combination of these three juices. We can say that modern physiology also supports the *Ayurvedic* approach of *Achha Pitta Nirman Kriya.* Due to these juices, all the fats and semi digested proteins are completely digested and converted in to fatty acids and glycerol and Amino acids.

(iii) Katu Avasthapaka:-

In this stage, the material passes down the *Pakvashaya* from the *Amashya* and being dried by *Agni,* and rendered in to lumps. *(Paripindita Pakva).* During this process *Vayu* and *Mala* are produced. In Modern physiology, the remaining materials are converted in to stools. The bacteria act on it and created some vitamins and indole and sketol like gases.

(B) Vipaka:-

According to *Charaka,* the digestion of food by *Jatharagni* breaks down the food in to five physicochemical groups viz *Parthiva, Aapya, Agneya, Vayavya* and *Akashiya.* Activated *Agni Mahabhuta* is present in each one of these *Bhautika* groups. The *Bhutagni* thus activates, digests the substances of that group. (*Ch. chi*-15/13)

(i) Bhutagni Paka:-

Bhutagni Paka follows *Jatharagni Paka* and it completes the process of intestinal digestion. After *Bhutagni Paka,* the *Ahara Rasa* is completed and the Rasa *Shoshana* is possible. Thus the *Agni* constituents of the predominantly *Parthiva* molecule spoken as *Parthivagni*, digest the substances of the molecules. Similarly *Apya Agni* gets the substance of the molecules of *Apya* and it for *Agneya, Vayavya,* and *Akashiya,* the out come of this type of digestion according to *Chakrapani* is the transformation of the characteristic qualities of each group and the assumption by them of *Vilakshana Gunas* or all together new qualities.

(ii) Dhatvagni Paka:-

After *Jatharagni Paka* & *Bhutagni Paka* of the *Ahara, Ahar Rasa* is created and it is absorbed from the *Annavaha Srotasa* and circulates throughout the body by *Dhamani,* this *Anna Rasa* undergoes the process of *Dhatvagni Vyapara* and thus *Saptadhatus* are created.

Seven different kinds of *Dhatvagnis* correspond to specific seven types of *Dhatus* viz *Rasagni, Raktagni, Mansagni, Medogni, Asthyagni, Majjagni* and *Shukragni.* The *Rasagni* does the digestion of the *Ahararasa,* so *Rasadhatu* and its *Mala* are developed. In the same process every *Dhatvagni* digests the same molecular particles of *Ahararasa* and same *Dhatu* is developed.

Acharya Charaka said that the *Dhatvagni* acts upon seven *Dhatus* giving rise to *Kitta* and *Prasada Bhaga.* (*Ch.Chi*-15/15).

The *Prasada Paka* is related to anabolic aspects and the *Kitta Paka* is of the catabolic. *Dhatvagni* converts the *Aharasa* in to *Sthayi* & *Asthayi Dhatu. Prasada Paka* is being an *Asthayi Dhatu. Asthayi Dhatu* is converted into *Sthayi Dhatu* by particular *Dhatvagni.* In *Dhatvagni Vyapara Kitta Paka* like *Sveda, Mutra, Purisha, Vata, Pitta, Kapha, Smashru, Nakha, Kesha* etc. are also developed.

Ayurved has given various concepts like *Khalekapota Nyaya, Ksheeradadhi Nyaya, Kedari Kulya Nyaya* etc. on *Dhatvagni Vyapara* or *Dhatu Nirman.*

3.4) <u>Historical Review:</u>

- ### *Vedic Kala:*

In Veda, there is no reference about *Amlapitta*.

- ### *Samhita Kala:*

(a) *Charaka Samhita:*

In *Charaka Samhita*, *Amlapitta* has not been described separately, but the word *"Amlapitta"* has been used at different places in *Sutrasthana* & *Chikitsasthana* which are as follows:

Ch.Su.1/111:   While describing the *Guna* and *Karma* of 8 types of milk, *Amlapitta* has bee listed as an indication.

Ch.Su.25/40:   *Kulattha* has been listed as the chief causative factor of *Amlapitta*.

Ch.Su.26/43 (3):   *Amlapitta* has been listed as a disease occurring due to excessive use of *Lavana Rasa*.

Ch.Su.26/103: Along with other diseases, *Amlapitta* has been listed as a disease caused by consuming *viruddha ahara.*

Ch.Su.27/25:   While describing the *Guna* and *Karma* of *Rajamasha*, it is said that *Rajamasha* is *Amlapitta roganashaka.*

Ch.Chi.7/148: *Amlapitta* has been listed as an indication of *Mahatiktaka Ghrita.*

Ch.Chi.12/52: *Amlapitta* has been listed as an indication of *Kansa Haritaki.*

Ch. Chi. 15/47: *Samprapti* of *Amlapitta* has been clearly mentioned here. According to *Charaka*, due to *Agnimandya* when the food is not digested properly, it forms *Annavisha* which when mixed with *Pitta* causes *Amlapitta.*

(b) *Sushruta samhita:*

In *Sushruta Samhita*, *"Amlapitta"* word has not been mentioned.

(c) *Kashyapa samhita:*

Amlapitta has been described separately in *Kashyapa Samhita*. It is the first *Samhita* describing the disease with its *Nidana, Rupa, Chikitsa* etc. Importance of *Desha* and *Kala* in *Amlapitta* has also mentioned in this *Samhita*.

(d) *Harita Samhita:*

Amlahikka word has been given for *Amlapitta* and is described in separate chapter.

- ### *Sangraha Kala:*

Urdhvag Amlapitta - Hetu & Nidanparivarjan   Dr. Parag Kulkarni & Dr. Amar Abhrange

(a) *Ashtanga sangraha & Hridaya:*

Amlika and *Amlaka* words are mentioned but *Amlapitta* has not been described in both texts.

(b) *Madhava Nidana:*

It is the first *Sangrahagrantha* which has detail description of *Amlapitta* along with its *Nidana, Rupa, Prakara, Samprapti,* etc.

(c) *Chakradutta:*

Detail *Chikitsa* of *Amlapitta* has been given in this text.

(d) *Sharangadhara Samhita*:

Sharangadhara has not described *Amlapitta* but he has mentioned its *Chikitsa* and preparatory methods of different types of recipes useful in *Amlapitta.*

(e) *Bhavaprakasha:*

The separate chapter of *Amlapitta* have been described in this text. *Upadrava & Arishta* has also been explained in this *Grantha.*

(f) *Yogaratnakara*:

Description of *Amlapitta* is just like *Madhava Nidana* but some more *Upadrava* are added in it.

(g) *Bangasen Samhita*:

This text contains detail description *of Amlapitta* along with its *chikitsa.*

(h) *Siddhanta Nidana*:

Amlapitta has been described in detail according to modern medicine. *Upadrava* are also mentioned.

(i) *Bhaishajya Ratnavali*:

Detail *Chikitsa* containing more effective *yoga* has been described in this text.

- ### *NIRUKTI*

The word *Amlapitta* etymologically comprises of two words **Amla** and **Pitta**. The word *Amla* has been used to express one among the six *rasas*. *Amla* is derived from:

अम्ल = अम् + क्ल् + अच् प्रत्यय ।

The word *Pitta* is derived from:

पित्तम् = अपि + दो त अपे: अकारलोपः ।
तप सन्तापे । तप दाहे । तप ऐश्वर्ये ।

(संस्कृत हिंदी शब्दकोष आपटे.)

The above quotations refer to heat, to burn, and the factors which are responsible to make one to achieve the eight kinds of benefits.

- ### *PARIBHASHA*

अम्लगुणोद्रिक्तम पित्तं अम्लपित्तम । (मा.नि. / अम्लपित्त /१)

The *Pitta* which becomes *Vidagdha* due to increase of *Amla Guna* of *Pitta*.

Amlapitta is condition where *Avipaka, Klama, Utlkesha, Tiktodgara, Amlodgara, Gourava, Hritdaha, Kanthadaha* and *Aruchi* are seen.

In a particular disease where *Amla* property of *Pitta* is increased along with *Pitta* is defined as *Amlapitta*.

Amlapitta is disease where *Pitta* leads to sour taste (*Amlabhavana*) and in such state whatever the food eaten is converted into *amlarasa*.

According to *Acharya Kashyapa*, the *Vidagdha Ahara* becomes *Amla* and remains still in the stomach which provocates the *Pitta Dosha*. Provocated *Pitta* causes reduction in the digestive power and also causes fermentation of the food. This fermented food in turn causes provocation of *Pitta* and vitiation of stomach, ultimately causing *"Amlapitta"*.

- ***PARYAYA NAMA***

Different classics have mentioned different names for the disease. These are tabulated as follows.

Table No-1

Shows *Paryayanamas* according different authors

PARYAYANAMA	*CH*	*SU*	*A.S.*	*K.S.*	*Y.R.*	*H.S.*	*M.N.*
Prameelaka	-	-	-	+	-	-	
Pittavisuchika	-	-	-	+	-	-	
Amlapitta	-	-	-	+	+	+	+
Pittamla	-	-	-	-	+		
Shuktaka	-	-	-	-	+		
Amlika	+	+	+	-	-	+	
Amlahikka	-	-	-	-	-		
Amlaka	+	+	+				

<u>**3.5) *Amlapitta – Ayurvedic* Review:**</u>

- <u>***NIDAN (HETU)***</u>

1) विरुद्धदुष्टशम्लविदाहि पित्तप्रकोपिपानान्नभुजो विदग्धम ।

पित्तं स्वहेतूपचितं पुरा यत्तदम्लपित्तं प्रवदन्ति सन्तः ।।

(मा.नि./अम्लपित्त /१)

(भा.प्र.१०/१)

(यो.र./अम्ल /१)

2) विरुद्धाध्यशनाजीर्णादामे आमे च पूरणात ।

पिष्टान्नामपक्वानां मद्यांना गोरसस्य च ।

गुर्वभिष्यन्दिभोज्यानां वेगानां धारणस्य च ।

अत्युष्णस्निग्धरुक्षाम्लद्वाणामतिसेवनात ।

फ़ाणितेक्षुविकाराणां कुलत्थानां च शिलनात ।

भुष्टधान्यपुलाकानां पृथुकानां तथैव च ।

भुक्त्वा भुक्त्वा दिवास्वप्नादतिस्नानावगाहनात ।

अंतरोदकपानाच्च भुक्तपर्युषिताशनात ।

-(का.खि. १६/१-६)

3) आनूपदेशे प्रायेण संभवत्त्वत्येश देहिनाम । -(का.खि. १६)

4) गुडनिषेवणाच्चाम्ले विरुध्दाहारसूचिते ।

कुपितंचाम्ल पित्तंच कंठस्तेन विदह्यते ।।

-(हा.सं.तृ. २४/१)

Nidana means the causative factors which leads to the disease. According to different *Ayurvedic* classics the *Nidanas* of A*mlapitta* can be classified as:

1)   *Aharaja.*   2) *Viharaja.*   3) *Manasika.*

Table No-2

Shows the _Aharaja, Viharaja, Manasika and Hetu_

AHARAJA	_VIHARAJA_	_MANASIKA_
Abhojana	_Bhukte bukte snana_	_Chinta_
Atibhojana	_Bhukte bukte avagaha_	_Shoka_
Ajeerna	_Bhukte bukte divaswapa_	_Krodha_
Amapurana	_Vegadharana_	_Bhaya_
Vishamashansana		
Adhyasana		
Gurubhojana		
Gorasatisevana		
Phanita-atisevana		
Pishta-atisevana		
Ikshuvikara atisevana		
Ushna atisevana		
Katurasa atisevana		
Amla rasa atisevana		
Drava atisevana		
Kulattha atisevana		
Madya atisevana		
Ruksha atisevana		
Bhrustadhanya atisevana		

Table No-3

Shows the _Samanya Hetu_ of _Amlapitta_ according to different classical texts

HETU	_CS_	_SH_	_AS_	_KS_	_MN_	_BP_	_YR_
Adhyashana	-	-	-	+	-	-	-
Ajeerna	+	-	-	+	+	-	-
Amapurna	-	-	-	+	-	-	-
Amla rasa atisevana	-	-	-	+	+	+	+
Atibhojana	-	-	-	+	+	+	+

Bhrista dhanya atisevana	-	-	-	+	-	-	-
Bhukte bhukte avagha	-	-	-	+	-	-	-
Bhukte bhukte snana	-	-	-	+	-	-	-
Bhukte bhukte divaswapa	-	-	-	+	-	-	-
Drava atisevana	-	-	-	+	-	-	-
Goras atisevana	-	-	-	+	-	-	-
Guda sevana	-	-	-	-	-	-	-
Guru bhojana	-	-	-	+	-	-	-
Ikshu vikara atisevana	-	-	-	+	-	-	-
Katu rasa atisevana	-	-	-		+	-	-
Kulattha atisevana	+		+	+	-	-	-
Lavana rasa atisevana	+	+		+	-	-	-
Madya atisevana	-	-	-	+	+	-	-
Phanita sevana	-	-	-	+	-	-	-
Pishta atisevana	-	-	-	+	-	-	-
Pitta prakopaka ahara & pana	-	-	-	-	+	+	+
Pruthuk atisevana	-	-	-	+	-	-	-

Ruksha atisevana	-	-	-	+	-	-	-
Snigdha atisevana	-	-	-	+	-	-	-
Takra sura	-	-	-		+	-	+
Ushna atisevana	-	-	-	+	-	-	-
Vikrut bhojana	-	-	-	+	+	+	+
Viruddha bhojana	-	-	-	+	+	+	+
Vishamashana	-	-	-	+	+	+	+

There are no direct references about the *Sannikrushta* and *Viprakrushta Hetu* of *Amlapitta*. Looking to the above table *Viruddha, Dustha, Amla, Vidahi, Pittaprakopa Annapana* etc. may be *Sannikrushta Hetu* and *Varsha Rutu* may be *Viprakrushta Hetu*.

- ### *PURVARUPA*

Ayurvedic classics have not mentioned the *Purvarupa* of *Amlapitta*. However the lower intensity of the symptoms may be considered as the *Purvarupa*.

- ### ***RUPA***

Rupa are those which are well manifested by which diseases are diagnosed. The *Rupa* of *Urdhvaga* and *Adhoga Amlapitta* have been explained separately in the classical texts along with the *Samanya Rupa*. While *Kashyapa* mentioned according to *Doshas*.

अम्लपित्त लक्षण:-

1) अविपाक क्लमोत्क्लेशतिक्ताम्लोद्वारगौरवैः ।
   हृत्कण्ठदाहारुचिभिश्वाम्लपित्तं वदेद्भिषक् ।
   (यो. र./अम्ल /२) (मा.नि./अम्ल/२) (भा.प्र.१०/२)

2) विड्भेदो गुरुकोष्ठत्वम्लोत्क्लेशः शिरोरुजा ।
   हृच्छूलमुदराध्मानमंगसादोल्न्त्रकूजनम् ।
   कण्ठोरसी विदहेते रोमहर्षश्च जायते ।
   -(का.सं.खि. १६/१४-१५)

3) दाहो वा हृदये तस्य शिरोऽर्तिश्चैव जायते ।
   उद्गारानम्लकान् कण्ठे हिक्काम्लोऽपि प्रधावति ।।
   -(हा.सं.तृ.स्थान २४/२)

Table No-4

Table shows *Lakshanas* according to different classics.

Laxanas	KS	MN	BP	YR	GN	RRS	SHS	HS
Adhamana	+	-	-	-	-	-	-	-
Amlodgara	+	+	+	+	+	+	+	+
Amlotklesha	+	-	-	-	-	-	-	-
Angasada	+	-	-	-	-	-	-	-
Antrakujana	+	-	-	-	-	-	-	-
Aruchi	-	+	+	+	+	+	-	-
Atisar	-	+	+	+	+	-	-	-
Avipaka	-	+	+	+	+	-	+	-
Vanti	-	+	+	+	+	-	-	-
Gourava	-	-	+	+	+	-	+	-
Gurukoshtha	+	-	-	-	-	-	-	-
Hikka	-	-	-	-	-	-	-	+
Hritdaha	+	+	+	+	+	+	+	+
Hritshoola	-	+	-	-	-	-	+	-
Kantha vidaha	+	+	+	+	+	-	+	+
Klama	-	+	+	+	+	-	-	-
Romaharsha	+	-	-	-	-	+	-	-

Shiroruk	+	-	-	-	-	-	-	+
Tiktodgara	-	+	+	+	+	+	+	-
Udgara	+	-	-	-	-	-	-	+
Urovidaha	+	-	-	-	-	-	-	-
Utklesha	-	+	+	+	+	-	-	-

- ## *VISHISHTA LAKSHANAS* OF *AMLAPITTA*

Kashyapa has explained three types of *Amlapitta.*

1. *Vataja*
2. *Pittaja*
3. *Kaphaja*

Table No-05

Table shows *vishista lakshanas* of *Amlapitta*

VATAJA	*PITTAJA*	*KAPHAJA*
Shoola	*Bhrama*	*Shareera guruta*
Angasada	*Vidaha*	*Vanti*
Jrumbha		

- ### ***BHEDA***

Different authors have classified *Amlapitta* under the following headings.

I)   According to *Dosha Samsarga.*

II)   According to *Gati.*

Table No-5

Showing the classification of *Amlapitta* according to different authors.

BHEDA	*KS*	*MN*	*BP*	*YR*	*GN*	*RRS*	*SH.S*	*HS*	*CHK*
Vataja	+	-	-	-	+	-	+	-	-
Kaphaja	+	-	-	-	-	-	+	-	-
Vata Kaphaj	-	-	-	+	+	-	+	-	-
Kapha pittja	-	-	-	+	+	-	-	-	-
Sanila	-	+	+	+	+	-	-	-	-
Sakapha	-	+	+	+	+	-	-	-	-
Sanila kapha	-	+	+	+	-	-	-	-	-
Urdhwaga	+	+	+	+	+	+	+	+	+
Adhoga	+	+	+	+	+	+	+	+	+

I)   <u>According to Dosha Samsarga:</u>

1. *Sanila / Vataj*

2. *Sanila kapha / Vata-Kaphaj*

3. *Sakapha / Kaphaj*

4. *Shleshma Pittaja / Kapha-Pittaj*

Sanila / Vataj

वातज अम्लपित्त लक्षण:-
कम्पप्रलपमूर्द्धाचिमिचिमिगात्रावसादशूलानि ।
तमसो दर्शनविभ्रमविमोहहर्षाण्यनिलकोपात् ।।
-(यो.र./अम्ल/८) -(भा.प्र.१०/८)

Aggravated *Piita* and *Vata Dosha* leads to *Agnimandya* which results in the *Shukta Paka* of *Ahara* and causes different symptoms as shown below:

Table No-6

Shows Sanila Amlapitta Lakshanas according to different classics

LAXANA	*MN*	*BP*	*YR*	*GN*
Tamo darshan	+	+	+	+
Shool	+	+	+	+
Gatravasaad	+	+	+	+
Moorcha	+	+	+	+
Kampa	+	+	+	+
Chimchimayan	+	+	+	+
Pralapa	+	+	+	+
Vibharama	+	+	+	+
Vimoha	+	+	+	+
Harsha	+	+	+	+

Sanila kapha / Vata-Kaphaj

वातकफज अम्लपित्त लक्षणे:-

सानिलं सानिलकफ सकफं तच्च लक्षयेत ।

दोष्लिन्गेन मतिमान्निष मोहकरं हि तत्त ।।

उभयमिदवेव चिन्हं मरुतकफसंभत्यम्ले ।

-(यो.र./अम्ल/१०)

-(मा.नि./अम्ल/११)

-(भा.प्र.१०/१०)

Vikruta Kapha and *VataDosha* located in *Amashaya* along with *Vikruta Pitta* results in *Agnimandya* which in turn causes *Shuktapaka,* and manifest with different symptoms like *Tiktodgara, Amlodgara, Katukodgara, Hritdaha, Kantha Daha, Kukshi Daha.*

Table No-7

Shows *Sanila kapha Amlapitta Lakshanas* according to different classics

LAXANA	*MN*	*BP*	*YR*
Tiktodgara	+	+	+
Amlodgara	+	+	+
Katukodgara	+	+	+
Hritkanthadaha	+	+	+
Kukshi daha	+	+	+

कफज अम्लपित्त लक्षणः-

कफनिष्ठीवनगौरवजडतारुचिशीतसादवमिलेपाः

दहनबलसादकण्डूनिद्राश्चिन्ह कफानुगते ।।

-(मा.नि./अम्ल/१०)

-(यो.र./अम्ल/९)

-(भा.प्र.१०/९)

Here *Kapha* contributes for the manifestation of symptoms as shown in the table:

Table No-8

Shows *Sakapha Amlapitta Lakshanas* according to different classics

LAXANA	MN	BP	YR	GN
Kaphasteevana	+	+	+	+
Vanti	+	+	+	+
Aruchi	+	+	+	+
Agnisada	+	+	+	+
Balasada	+	+	+	+
Angasada	+	+	+	+
Urdwagata	+	+	+	+
Jadata	+	+	+	+
Kandu	+	+	+	+
Nidra	+	+	+	+

कफपित्तज अम्लपित्त लक्षणः-

१) भ्रमोमूच्छोरुचिश्छर्दिरालस्यं च शिरोरुजा ।

प्रसेको मुखमाधुर्य श्लेष्मपित्तस्य लक्षणम्

-(यो.र./अम्ल/१२)

२) करचरणदाह मौष्ण्यं महतिमरुचिं ज्वरं च कफपित्तम्।

जनयति कण्डूमण्डलपिटीकाचित्तगात्ररोगचयम् ।।

-(यो.र.)

Here due to *kapha* and *Pitta Dosha* the different symptoms are seen.

Table No-9

Shows *Shleshma pittja Amlapitta Lakshanas* according to different classics

LAXANA	*YR*	*GN*
Shiroruk	+	+
Bhrama	+	+
Mukha madhuryata	+	+
Praseka	+	+
Aruchi	+	+
Tiktodgara	+	+
Amlodgara	+	+
Kanthadaha	+	+
Kukshidaha	+	+
Hritdaha	+	+
Alasya	+	+
Katukodgara	+	+
Moorcha	+	+
Tama	+	+
Vanti	+	+

II)   ACCORDING TO *GATI*:

1) *Urdhvag Amlapitta*

2) *Adhoga Amlapitta*

1) *Urdhvag Amlapitta*:

Due to *Nidana, Dosha* located in *Urdhva Amashaya* tend to have *Urdhva Gati* and symptoms like *Utklesha, Hrit-Kantha-Kuskhi Daha, Chhardi* and *Tikta-Amla Udgara* are produced.

उर्ध्वग अम्लपित्त लक्षणे-

वान्तं हरित्पीतकनीलकृष्णमारक्ताभमतीव चाम्लम् ।

मांसोदकाभं त्वतिपिच्छिलाच्छं श्लेष्मानुजातं विविधं रसेन् ।।

भुक्ते विदग्धे त्वथवाऽप्यभुक्ते करोति तिक्ताम्लवमिं कदाचित् ।

उद्गारमेवंविधिमेव कण्ठहृत्कुक्षिदाहं शिरसो रुजं च ।।

करचरणदाहमौष्ण्यं महतीमरुचिं ज्वरं च कफ़पित्तम् ।

जनयति कन्डूमण्डलपिडकाशतनिचितगात्ररोगचयम् ।।

-(मा.नि./अम्ल./४-६) -(यो.र./अम्ल/४-६) -(भा.प्र.१०/३)

Table No-10

Shows *Urdhvaga Amlapitta Lakshanas* according to different classics.

LAXANA	KS	MN	BP	YR	GN
Vantam hareetam	+	+	+	+	+
Vantam peetam	+	+	+	+	+
Vantam neelam	-	+	+	+	+
Vantam krishnam	+	+	+	+	+
Vantam araktam	+	+	+	+	+
Vantam raktabham	-	+	+	+	+
Vantam mamsodaka toyabham	-	+	+	+	+
Vantam atipicchilam	-	+	+	+	+

Vantam accham	-	+	+	+	+
Vantam shleshmanugatam	-	+	+	+	+
Rasesa vividham	-	+	+	+	+
Bukte vidagdhe tikta vami	-	+	+	+	+
Bhukte amlvami	-	+	+	+	+
Bhukte tiktodgara	-	+	+	+	+
Bhukte amlodgra	-	+	+	+	+
Kukshi daha	-	+	+	+	+
Kara daha	-	+	+	+	+
Charana daha	-	+	+	+	+
Ushnata	-	+	+	+	+
Jwara (kahpa pittaja)	-	+	+	+	+
Kandu	-	+	+	+	+
Pidaka	-	+	+	+	+
Shiroruja	+	+	+	+	+
Mandala	-	+	+	+	+
Kanthadaha	-	+	+	+	+
Avipaka	-	+	+	+	+

2) *Adhog Amlapitta:*

Due to *Nidana, Dosha* situated in *Adho Amashaya*; tend to have *Adhogati* and presents with *Nana Vidha Varnayukta Adhopravhana, Trishna, Daha, Moorchha, Agnisada, Kotha, Hrillasa, Bhrama, Moha, Sweda Pradurbhava* etc *Lakshana.*

अधोग अम्लपित्त लक्षणेः
तृड्दाह मूर्छा भ्रममोहकारि प्रत्यात्यधो वा विविधप्रकारम् ।
हृल्लासकोठानलसादहर्षस्वेदांगपीतत्वकरं कदाचित् ।।
-(मा.नि./अम्ल/३)
-(यो.र./अम्ल/३)
-(भा.प्र.१०/४)

Table No-11

Shows *Adhoga Amlapitta Lakshanas* according to different classics.

LAXANA	*KS*	*MN*	*BP*	*YR*	*GN*
Bhrama	+	+	+	+	+
Trishna	+	+	+	+	+
Hrillasa	+	+	+	+	+
Analasada	+	+	+	+	+
Nanavidha varna yukta pravahana	+	+	+	+	+
Anga peetata	+	+	+	+	+
Daha	+	+	+	+	+
Harsha	+	+	+	+	+
Sweda	+	+	+	+	+
Kotha	+	+	+	+	+
Moha	+	+	+	+	+
Moorcha	+	+	+	+	+

- ## *UPASHAYA –ANUPASHAYA*

Kashyapa explained the *upashaya for Amlapitta* as follows.

Vataja Amlapitta	– *Snigdha Ahara.*
Pittaja Amlapitta	– *Sheeta Ahara.*
Kaphaja Amlapitta	– *Ruksha Ahara.*

- ## *SAMPRAPTI*

अम्लपित्त संप्राप्ति

वातादयः प्रकुप्यन्ति तेषामन्यतमो यदा ।
मन्दिकरोति कायाग्निमग्नौ मार्दवमागते ।।
एतान्वेव तथा भूयः सेवमानस्य दुर्मतेः ।
यत्किंचिदशितं पीतं देहिनस्तद् हि दहति ।।
विदग्धं शुक्ततां याति शुक्तमामाशये स्थितम् ।
तदम्लपित्तमित्याहुर्भूयिष्ठं पित्तदूषणात् ।।

-(का.सं. १६/७-९)

Samprapti means description of physiological derangements and pathological processes, which take place in a person due to *Nidana Sevana.* It helps to understand the manifestation of clinical features and it also has therapeutic importance. The ancient scholars have stated that *Samprapti Vighatanameva Chikitsa,* that is, reversal of pathogenesis is the complete treatment.

Kashyapa elaborately explained about *Samprapti* of *Amlapitta.* Due to *Nidana Sevana Vatadi Doshas* become aggravated and it affects the *Agni* to produce *Jatharagni Mandya* and due to the *Agni Mandya; Aharras* attains *Vidagdhata.* This *Vidagdha Amarasa* later undergoes *Shuktapaka* in *Amashaya.* In this stage if the person consumes anything due to *Jatharagni Mandya* it becomes vitiated due to *Vidagdha Pitta* and produces *Amlapitta.*

Madhavakara in his *Madhava Nidana* explains *Samprapti* as; *Pitta,* which is already *Sanchita* due to its self-aggravating factors, further, attains *Vidagdhata* due to *Virudha Ahara* (incompatible diet), *Dusta, Amla, Vidahi* and *Pitta provocating* food and drinks.

<h1 style="text-align:center"><u>Schematic presentation of Samprapti of Amlapitta</u></h1>

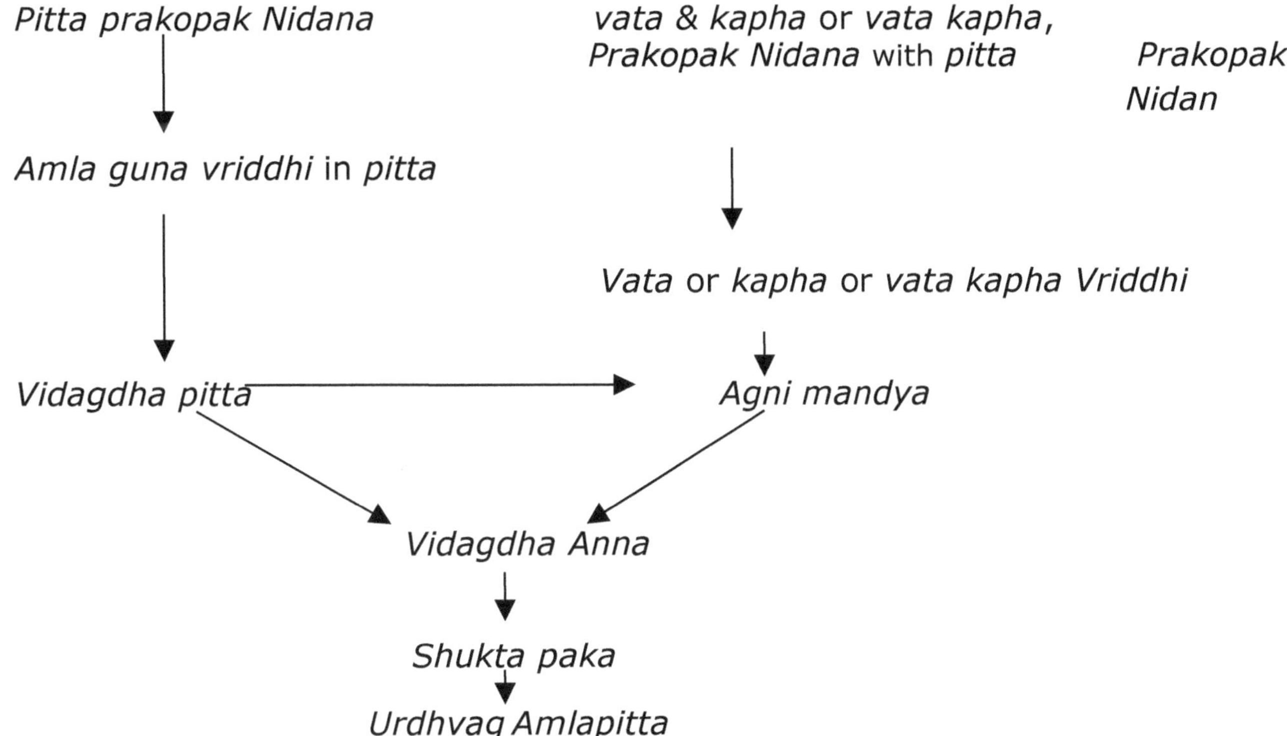

Due to the *Pitta prakopak nidana sevana*, especially *amla guna vardhaka ahara*, the *amla guna* of *Pitta* increases and it is called as *vidagdha Pitta*, which leads to *Agni mandya*, i.e., *jatharagni mandya*.

If the person indulges in *vatakara* or *kaphakara* or both *vata* and *kaphakaraka nidana* along with above said *nidana*, then also contribute for *agni mandya* i.e. *jataragni mandya*.

Due to the *vidagdha Pitta* and *jatharagni mandya* the *shuktha paka of ahara* takes place in *amashaya*.

In these stages if he consumes further more *nidanakaraka ahara;* more *shuktha paka* will take place. This stage is called as *Amlapitta*.

As a result, *dusta ama*, i.e. *shuktha paka* accumulates or formed in *annavaha Srotas* mainly in *amashaya* and produce symptoms.

The *samprapti* of *vidagdhajeerna* is similar but in *Amlapitta* the type of abnormalities persists continuously or intermittently for longer time with consumption of *nidanakara ahara vihara*.

Thus the difference between *vidagdhajeerna* and *Amlapitta* is in its *chronicity* and its course. Vidagdhajeerna is an acute condition of short duration and *Amlapitta* is the chronic disorder of prolonged course. Due to this reason, in *Brihatrayee*; concept of *Amlapitta* might have been included in *Ajeerna*.

- ### <u>*Samprapti* according to the *shatkriyaKala:*</u>

1)   Sanchaya:

Varsha Ritu, Anupa Desha, Vidahi Annapana, Amla–Katu Sevana, Dravadhikya etc. will cause *Pitta Vriddhi* and this leads to *Agnidushti. Pitta Prakriti* of the persons may also interfere in this condition. This stage is called as *Sanchaya Avastha.* Due to *Nidana Sevana Kapha* and *Vata* also gets vitiated. In this stage *Nidana Parivarjana* is only the treatment for promotion of the health.

2)   Prakopa:

Due to excessive *Nidana Sevana Pitta* is more provoked and *Sanchita Pitta* becomes *Prakupita.* This stage is called the *Prakopa Avastha.* In this *Agnimandya* and *Ajirna* are produced and the symptoms like *Avipaka, Amlodgara, Daha* etc. are produced. Due to *Ajirna, Shuktpaka of anna* leads to the production of the *Annavisha.* In this stage the treatment is *Nidana Parivarjana, Deepana* and *Pachana Karma.*

3)   Prasara:

The *Annavisha* circulate in the body with the help of *Ahara Rasa* and *Dhamanis,* so *Rasa Dhatu* is also vitiated. This *Annavisha* is mixed with *Pitta Dosha* and circulates into the whole body. This stage may differentiate like *Amajirna, Vidagdhajirna* and *Vishtabdhajirna* due to involvement of with *Visharupa Annapana.* It is also noted that *Manovaha Srotas* gets vitiated due to excessive manifestation of various mental factors causing symptoms of *Ajirna* and *Amlapitta.* In this *Amapachana* with *Tikta-Madhura Dravya, Langhana* and *Nidana Parivarjana* are suitable.

4)   Sthana Sanshraya:

This is the forth stage and from here the specific pathogenesis of each disease starts according to the specificity of *Nidanas.* Quality of *Dosha* by which they are vitiated and the place of *Khavaigunya.* So, the three *Dosha- Samanavayu, Pachaka Pitta* and *Kledaka Kapha* may get *Sthana Sanshrita* in *Amashaya* (including *Grahani*) where simultaneously *Khavaigunya* might have been produced by the same *Nidana* or by any other *Nidana.* The symptoms produced in this stage may be same as *Symptomatology* of the *Amlapitta* and having less severity. If treatment is not done in this stage the pathogenesis may proceed further and may produce the disease like *Parinama Shula.*

This is the stage from where the *Vidagdhajirna* can be separated from *Amlapitta. Vidagdhajirna* is an acute stage occurring due to *nidanas* directly. And is *Nidana Sapeksha,* which means after the *Mithya Ahara-Vihara* or *Pittaprakopak* diet articles will lead to *Vidagdhajirna,* but here the *Dosha* have not established their affinity with any organ on tissue and only *Langhana* or time will cure the condition, but symptoms may be produced again and again whenever the *Mithya Ahara* and *Vihara* will be done. But due to again and again provocation, the *Dosha* will establish their affinity in *Amashaya* and *Grahani (Sthanasamshraya)*. After this stage even the *Laghu* and *Alpa Bhojana* will cause *Shuktapak* and *Vidagdhata* to *Annapana* leading to the production of *Amlapitta Roga*.

5)   *Vyakti:*

In *sthana samshraya Pitta dhara Kala* or *grahani* is vitiated by the *sama Pitta.*

The vitiated *Pitta* gets *kha-vaigunya*. At this stage the symptoms of the disease may get well established and further differentiation in the *Doshic* varieties according to the predominance like *vataja, kaphaja* and *vatakaphaja* can be done. *Madhavakar* has also given a separate classification according to the expulsion route of i.e.

urdhvaga and *adhoga* type.

6)   *Bheda:*

When the disease progresses further it reaches to the sixth stage. Due to the manifestation of the various symptoms, the disease can be categorized as *Vatika, Vatashleshmika* or *Shleshma-Pitta* as described by *Madhavakara*. Due to further involvement of *Vata* and *Rakta,* the disease can produce *Parinama Shula*, as an *Upadrava* or as *Nidanarthakaratva*.

1] *Sankhya Samprapti* -

    a. Two types according to *gati.*

        i. *Urdhvaga*

        ii. *Adhoga*

    b. Three types according to *Kashyap*

        i. *Vatolbana*

        ii. *Pittolbana*

        iii. *Kapholbana*

    c. Three types according to *Madhavakara*

        i. Vatika

        ii. *Vata kapha*

        iii. Kapha

        iv. Also counted fourth types as *shleshma Pitta*

2] *Vidhi Samprapti* –

    a.   i. *Nija*   ii. *Agantuka*

    b.   *i. Svatantra*   *ii. Paratantra*

    c.   According to curability –

        i. *Naveena* - curable by tactful treatment

        ii. *Chirothita - krichhra sadhya*

        iii. *Chirothita - yapya*

3] *Vikalpa Samprapti* –

    a. *Vata - Chala, Ruksha, Karmatah*

    b. *Pitta - Dravyatah, Ushma, Tikshna, Sara, Amla, Katu, Drava*

    c. *Kapha - Dravyatah, Karmatah, Guru, Mridu.*

4] *Pradhanya Samprapti* –

    a. *Pitta - Vriddhatama*

    b. *Kapha - Vriddhatara*

    c. *Vata – Vriddha*

5] *Bala – Kala vishesha* -

    a. Seasonal aggravation   i. *Sharada*   ii. *Greeshma*

b. Day/ night   i. Noon   ii. Mid-night

c. Dietetic time   i. *Bhojanottara*

6] *Anshansha Kalpana –*

In the pathogenesis of *Amlapitta,* first there is production of *Shuktapaka* due to Agni *dushti* and if it mixes with *Pitta* it produces the disease. Means along with excessive HCl secretion there may be production of organic acids. So whenever patients complain about hyperacidity, his thorough examination as per *Ayurvedic* point of view should be done. We must analyze by which property *Pitta* is vitiated and mixed with *Shuktapaka*, as treatment differs in these situation.

Mainly Drava and *Amla Gun*a is increased in this disease. By observing the sign and symptoms of patients, we can guess by which *Guna* (property*) Pitta* is vitiated which is described here.

Guna –   *Lakshana* (Symptoms)

Drava -   *Hrillas, Asyastravana, Chhardi*

Amla -   *Amlika, Amlasyata, Amlodgara, Amlarasayukta Chhardi*

Tikshna -   *Vedana, Vrana (ulcer)*

Ushna - *Ura-Udara-KanthaDaha, Jwaraprachiti, sarvangadaha*

Vistra -   *Aasya-daurgandhya, Loha-Ama Gandha, Utsahahani*

Sara -   *Asamhat mala pravrutti*

By analyzing these *Guna* we can change the line of treatment accordingly.

If we are able to differentiate these properties then we can treat the patient easily and get better result.

Likewise if these properties involved different *Dhatu* then also we can change line of treatment and it should be according to progression of pathogenesis.

Samprapti ghataka of *Urdhvag Amlapitta:*

1.	*Dosha*	:	*Pitta Pradhana Kapha.*
2.	*Dushya*	:	*Rasa Dhatu.*
3.	*Agni*	:	*Jatharagni.*
4.	*Ama*	:	*Jatharagnijanya Ama.*
5.	*Srotas*	:	*Annavaha And Rasavaha.*
6.	*Srotodusti Prakara*	:	*Sanga, Vimarga-Gamana.*

Urdhvag Amlapitta - Hetu & Nidanparivarjan   Dr. Parag Kulkarni & Dr. Amar Abhrange

7.   *Udbhava Sthana*   :   *Amashaya.*

8.   *Adhisthana*   :   *Amashaya.*

9.   *Sanchara Sthana*   :   *Mahasrotas.*

10.   *Vyakta Sthana*   :   *Amashaya.*

11.   *Rogamarga*   :   *Abhyantara.*

- ### *SADHYASADHYATA*

रोगोऽयमम्लपित्ताख्यो यत्नात् संसाध्यते नवः ।

चिरोत्थितो भवेद्याप्यः कृच्छ्रसाध्यः स कस्यचित् ।।

-(मा.नि./अम्ल/७)

Before going to start the *Chikitsa* of a particular disease, one should know about the *Sadhyasadhyata* of a disease, i.e. whether it is easily curable, curable with efforts or incurable etc. should be known. According to *Prabhava,* the diseases are classified as *Sadhya* and *Asadhya. Sadhya* is subdivided as *Sukha Sadhya* and *Krichra Sadhya, Asadhya* is subdivided as *Yapya* and *Pratyakhya.*

In case of *Amlapitta, Nava Amlapitta* is curable with efforts. When it becomes chronic, it is considered to be *Krichra Sadhya* or *Yapya* in persons those who adopt proper *Pathya-Apathya.* If *Amlapitta* is associated with complications it is considered as *Yapya* or *Asadhya.*

- ### *SAPEKSHA NIDANA*

One should properly examine the patient and come to a proper conclusion before starting the treatment in all the diseases. *Sapeksha Nidana* is nothing but differential diagnosis of disease. One should properly distinguish the disease from other diseases, which are having same signs and symptoms.

The disease which are having similar signs and symptoms as that of *Amlapitta* are as follows:

1.   *Vidagdhaajeerna.*

2.   *Pittaja Shoola.*

3.   *Parinama Shoola.*

4.   *Annadrava Shoola.*

5.   *Pittaja Gulma.*

1. *Vidagdhaajeerna* and *Amlapitta* :

Some of the symptoms such as *Bhrama, Moorcha, Vividha Ruja* of *Pitta* like *Osha, Chosha* etc *Dhumodgara, Amlodgara, Sweda, Daha* etc may be seen in both disorders.

The difference between these two diseases is only in its chronicity and course. *Vidagdhajeerna* is acute in nature. Some prominent symptoms of *Amlapitta* such as *Hrid-Daha, Kukshidaha, Amlachhardi, Aruchi, Udarashoola, Atisara* are not seen in *Vidagdhajeerna*. *Vidagdhajeerna* is due to *PittaDosha* only while *Amlapitta* although due to *Pitta* as prominent *Dosha*, but the others two *Dosha* i.e. *Vata* and *Kapha* will be accompanied.

2. *Pittaja shoola* and *Amlapitta:*

Teevra Shoola, Trishna, Moorcha, Mutradaha,Swedapradurbhava, Bhrama, Chosha are the main symptoms of *Pittaja Shoola*. Here *shoola* is *Teevra* in nature and at *Nabhi*. The time for aggravation of *Shoola* will be noon, midnight and during the course of digestion. While in *Amlapitta, Shoola* is *Manda* and *Dahayukta* and at *Amashaya* and not concerned to the time period.

3. *Parinaam shoola* and *amlapiita:*

Parinaam Shoola is associated with *Adhmana, Vibandha, Atopa, Trishna, Atisweda Lakshana*. Here the *Shoola* relieves by intake of food, after the digestion and by inducing *Vamana Karma*. By these features it will be differentiated with *Amlapitta*.

4. *Annadrava shoola* and *Amlapitta:*

In *Annadrava Shoola*, the *shoola* is continuously persisting unrelated to the intake of *Ahara* and only relieves by *Vamana Pittanirgamana*. But in *Amlapitta* though *Shoola* is one of the symptoms, along with this *Hridaha, Kuskhidaha, Kanthadaha, Amlodgara* etc are the main symptoms seen. Thus it can be differentiated.

5. *Pittaja Gulma* and *Amlapitta:*

In *Pittaja Gulma; Daha, Amlata, Moorcha, Vitbheda, Sweda, Trishana, Jwara* are found. In addition it will also have *Haridrata* in skin, eyes, urine etc are described; which are not described in *Amlapitta.*

- ## *UPADRAVA*

Kashyap has mentioned ***Upadrava*** of ***Amlapitta*** as follows:

अम्लपित्त उपद्रव :

ज्वरातिसारपांडु त्वशूलशोथारुचिभ्रमैः ।
उपद्रवैरिमैर्जुष्टः क्षिणधातुर्न सिध्यति ।।
-(काश्यप संहिता)

- ➢ *Jwara*
- ➢ *Atisara*
- ➢ *Panduta*
- ➢ *Shoola*
- ➢ *Shotha*
- ➢ *Aruchi*
- ➢ *Bhrama*

1) आम्लपित्ते प्रयोक्तव्या कफपित्तहरो विधि ।

गुड कूष्मांडकं चैव तथा खंडामलक्यापि ।।

-(यो.र./अम्ल)

2) यवगोधूममुद्राश्च पुरणा रक्तशालयः ।

जलानि तप्तशीतानि शर्करा मधु सक्तवः ।।

कर्कोटकं काखेल्ल् रंभापुष्पं च वास्तुकम्।।

वेतग्रम् कुद्धकूष्माण्डं पटोलं दाडिमं तथा।।

पानान्नानि समस्तानि कफपित्तहराणि च।

आम्लपित्तामये नित्यं सेवितव्यानि मानवैः।।

-(यो.र./अम्ल)

The term *Pathya* means that which is compatible to health and which is not conductive to health is called as *Apathya*. Disease can be cured only by adopting *pathya* or wholesome regimen. But without following *Pathya*, which comprises of wholesome *Ahara-Vihara* and *Charya*, any amount of medicine may not help in curing the disease.

The following is the *Pathya* stated in *Amlapitta*, it *is Laghu Bhojana, Shalidhanya, Yava, Godhuma, Mudgayusha, Lajasaktu.*

The *Jangala Mamsa Rasa, Kalayashakha, Godugdha, Goghrita, Mudga,* other than these which are drugs having *Tikta Rasa* and *Laghu* property. Those drugs which does not produce *Vidaha* property and the foods or activities which are *Satmya* to the body are considered as *Pathya. Tiktarasa Pradhana Ahara* and *Paneya* are more benifical in *Amlapitta.*

Other than this *Karkota, Karavellka, Patola, Kushmanda, Vastuka, Kapitta, Dadima,* and other bitters; all sorts of food and drinks having the property of pacifying *Kapha* and *Pitta* are considered as *Pathya* and *Prakopaka Ahara* and *Vihara;* excess use of *Tila, Masha, Kulattha, Taila, Dhanyamla, Brista Dhanya, Madya* and *Rasas* like *Amla, Lavana, Katu* are considered as *Apathya.*

Above mentioned *apathyas* shows that:

(1) The drugs which are provoking *Pitta Dosha*

(2) The drugs which increase, *Kapha Dosha* and vitiates the *Agni* are considered as *Apathya* for *Amlapitta.*

Urdhvag Amlapitta - Hetu & Nidanparivarjan   Dr. Parag Kulkarni & Dr. Amar Abhrange

Kashyap suggests change of place or environment and rehabilitation in view to protect life for four fold achievement.

3.6) *Amlapitta* - Modern Aspect:

In modern medical science, much disease can be correlated with *Amlapitta*. But the signs and symptoms of "Hyperacidity" are similar to that of *Amlapitta*.

Hyperacidity literally means 'excess of acid' or 'hyper-secretion of acid from stomach', when taken in relation to GIT.

Hyperactivity is a functional and a very common dietary disorder of the digestive system. The human stomach secrets HCl which is necessary for the digestion of the food substances. HCl breakdowns the food particles in their minute form. The oxyntic cells of stomach secrete HCl. Acetylcholine stimulates all gastric glands to secrete HCl. Gastrin and Histamine strongly stimulates the parietal cells to secrete HCl. Deficiency of secretin increases secretion of HCl. Strong emotional stimuli frequently increases the acid secretion. The excessive secretion of acid in the stomach leads to formation of ulcer.

- ### CAUSES OF HYPERACIDITY :

1. Irregular dietary habits

2. Excessive intake of oily, spicy and highly seasoned food like chilly, pickles, etc.

3. Excessive intake of sour foods that contain high acid content

4. Going to bed immediately after a heavy meal

5. Loss of appetite

6. Inadequate exercise

7. Too much mental stress and worries

8. Taxing the mind excessively

9. Insomnia

10. Prolonged alcohol ingestion

11. Heavy smoking and drug addiction

12. Prolonged ingestion of aspirin or some anti inflammatory drugs

13. Diseases of the digestive organs such as the stomach, intestines, gallbladder or the pancreas

14. Peptic ulcers

15. Spinal lesions

16. Blood group 'O'

17. Idiopathic

18. Also occurs after surgery or burns or with severe bacterial infection

- **<u>SYMPTOMS OF HYPERACIDITY :</u>**

1. A steady pain of short duration in upper abdomen immediately following a large or spicy meal or aspirin ingestion

2. A typical feeling of restlessness

3. Nausea, vomiting, and loss of desire to eat which may persist for 1-2 days

4. Heart burn or sour belching with an aftertaste of the already-eaten food

5. Early repletion or satiety after meals

6. A sense of abdominal distension or 'bloating'

7. Flatulence (burping, belching)

8. Stiffness in the stomach

9. Vomiting of blood or blood in stools

10. Indigestion

11. Constipation

12. If gastritis persists there may be eventual development of anaemia Long-standing hyperacidity may lead to formation of ulcers in the stomach which may again lead to complications like perforation.

<u>Correlation between Hyperacidity and *Amlapitta* :</u>

Hyperacidity	***Amlapitta***
Heart burn	*Hritdaha*
Chest pain	*Hritshoola*
Abdominal distension	*Udar aadhmana*
Sour belching	*Amlodgara*

Acid refluxes of the food taken	*Amlotklesha*
Loss of appetite	*Aruchi*

- ## **COMPLICATIONS OF HYPERACIDITY :**

Several digestive complications are known to be caused due to prolonged hyperacidity. The following are some of them –

(1) Chronic gastritis

(2) Gastric ulcers

(3) Heartburn

Hyperacidity is generally a simple condition that can be resolved by some simple medication. However, in certain types of people, this situation becomes more complicated. Hyperacidity is more dangerous in people if:

1. They are above fifty years of age.

2. They are trying to lose weight below the normal values.

3. They are suffering from anorexia.

4. The hyperacidity condition is continuing for more than two weeks.

5. There is a feeling of some mass in the stomach.

- ## **PREVENTION OF HYPERACIDITY :**

Hyperacidity can be taken care of with a strict and healthy dietary routine. The following principles must be observed:

(1) A person with hyperacidity problems must totally abstain from consuming heavy food.

(2) It is very important to perform some light exercise after every meal in order to burn some   calories. Alternatively, the person can go on a brisk walk.

(3) Smoking and alcoholism must be totally avoided by people having repeated complaints of hyperacidity.

(4) The mind should be kept free and devoid of tensions during eating.

(5) One should be refrained from unnecessary medication.

- ### <u>DIET DURING HYPERACIDITY :</u>

Hyperacidity is caused by indigestion. Hence, a proper hyperaciditydiet is the most proper way to get the disease treated. The following dietary regimen must be followed by people to get their hyperacidity treated:

(1) The diet must be *Pitta* pacifying and contain more of bitter and astringent tastes. Salads and legumes must be included in the diet.

(2) Foods that are difficult to digest must be avoided. This includes salty, oily and spicy foods.

(3) Sour foods like tamarind, lemons, curds, etc. must be avoided.

(4) The intake of pulses must be avoided.

(5) The food must be properly cooked, but not overcooked, in order to aid digestion.

- ### <u>MANAGEMENT OF HYPERACIDITY :</u>

(1) Managed by relieving the causative factors.

(2)Drugs like antacids, H_2 receptor antagonists, proton pump Inhibitors, prokinetics, anticholinergics and antibiotics.

(3) Psycho therapy if needed.

(4) Surgery in advanced stage.

<u>SOME OTHER CONDITIONS:</u>

1) <u>Gastritis:</u>

It refers to the inflammatory condition of the gastric mucosa. There are many clinical types of gastritis, but they are divided into

1. Acute Gastritis

2. Chronic Gastritis

<u>Acute Gastritis:</u>

Acute gastritis is characterized by -

- Epigastric pain

- Nausea and vomiting

- Anorexia

- Massive haematemesis

Chronic gastritis is characterized by the absence of grossly visible mucosal erosion. But chronic inflammatory changes may lead to mucosal atrophy.

Although, usually it is asymptomatic, but it may be associated with Pernicious Anaemia, Gastric ulcer, duodenal ulcer and Gastric carcinoma.

Types on histological basis:

Type A - Body and fundus of stomach is involved

- Less common

- Auto immune in origin

- Asymptomatic

- Gastric cancer chances are high

Type B - Antrum of stomach is involved

- Helicobacter pylori is the causative agent

Common causes of Gastritis:

➢ Acute gastritis (often erosive and haemorrhagic)

➢ Aspirin, NSAIDs

➢ H. Pylori (initial infection)

➢ Alcohol

➢ Drugs e.g. iron preparation

➢ Severe physiological stress, e.g. burns, multi organ failure

➢ Bile reflux e.g. following gastric surgery

Urdhvag Amlapitta - Hetu & Nidanparivarjan   Dr. Parag Kulkarni & Dr. Amar Abhrange

➤ Viral infection e.g. cytomegalovirus (CMV), herpes simplex

<u>Chronic non-specific Gastritis:</u>

➤ H. pylori infection

➤ Auto immune (Pernicious Anaemia)

➤ Post gastrectomy

<u>Chronic specific forms (rare):</u>

➤ Infections, e.g. CMV, tuberculosis

➤ Gastrointestinal disease e.g. Crohn's disease

➤ Idiopathic e.g. granulomatouos gastritis

2)   <u>Peptic ulcer:</u>

An ulcer in the lower oesophagus, stomach, duodenum and in the jejunum after surgical anastomosis to the stomach.

Causative factors are -

1. NSAIDs

2. Alcohol

3. Iron

4. Antimitotic agents

5. Bile reflux

6. Severe mental stress

7. Uraemia

8. Helicobacter pylori

9. Type 'A' gastritis - autoimmune

10. Intact stomach - Helicobacter pylori

11. Eosinophilic gastritis allergy

12. Chronic stress

13. Corticosteroids

14. Duedenogastric reflux of bile

15. Disorders of gastric emptying like slow emptying, fast emptying

Clinical features:

1. Recurrent abdominal pain which is associated with the following

Features:

i) Epigastric pain   ii) Hunger pain

iii) Night pain   iv) Periodic pain

2. Water brash

3. Heart burn

4. Loss of appetite

5. Vomiting

Investigations:

1. Double contrast Barium meal

2. Endoscopy

3. Biopsy of gastric mucosa

4. Stool routine and gastric analysis: for detection of blood in stool or

   gastric aspirate in acute gastritis respectively.

3)   Dyspepsia:

Indigestion is a collective term for non specific symptoms thought to have originated from the upper gastrointestinal tract.

Symptoms:

1.   Upper abdominal pain or lower chest pain with or without relation to food

2.   Regurgitation (gastro-oesophageal)

3.   Heart burn

4.   Water brash

5.   Anorexia

6.   Vomiting

7.   Nausea

8.   Bloating, belching, flatulence

9. Early repletion (satiety after meal)

4) Non ulcer dyspepsia (functional):

It comprises of a spectrum of mucosal motility and psychiatric disorders.

Urdhvag Amlapitta - Hetu & Nidanparivarjan   Dr. Parag Kulkarni & Dr. Amar Abhrange

Clinical features:

1. Young patients < 40 years
2. Women to men ratio 2:1
3. Abdominal pain
4. Nausea
5. Bloating after meals
6. Sense of incomplete bowel evacuation

5) Irritable bowel syndrome:

• Functional disorder

• Abdominal pain associated with disordered defecation

• Psychological factors like anxiety, stress depression may be the underlying cause

• Episodes of diarrhoea and constipation

• Abdominal discomfort

• Dyspepsia

• Chronic fatigue syndrome.

6) Peptic ulcer disease (Gastric and Duodenal ulcer)

• Chronic condition with a natural history of spontaneous relapse and remission

• Recurrent abdominal pain

• Epigastric pain

• Hunger pain

• Episodic pain

• Heart burn

• Water brash

• Vomiting

• Loss of appetite

• Nausea

Although Duodenal and Gastric ulcers are different disease, they share common symptoms, which are considered above.

As explained earlier, any disease does not perfectly correlate with the aetiology, signs and symptomatology of *Amlapitta*. Some diseases show similarity in the causes, some in the signs and some share common symptoms with *Amlapitta*.

4) <u>Material and Methods:</u>

4.1) <u>Material:</u>

1) Selection of Patients-

2) Selection & Preparation of drug-

4.2) <u>Methods:</u>

1) Aims of Study-

2) Literature Review-

3) Plan of Work for Clinical Study-

I) Diagnostic phase.
II) Interventional Phase.
III) Assessment phase.

4.1) <u>Material:</u>

<u>1) Selection of Patients-</u>

Selection of patients is done randomly as per rules of statistics. For present study, patients are selected from-

1) Patients from *Rognidan* OPD & IPD

2) Volunteers from college & hospital premises

3) Patients in medical camps organized by college & hospital authorities.

4) Study was carried out after appropriate counseling of the patients and informed written consent from the patients.

➢ **<u>Inclusion Criteria -</u>**

1.   Patients of both sexes are selected.

2.   Patients suffering from signs and symptoms of *Urdhvag Amlapitta* for more than 7 days were selected for the study.

3.   Patients of Age group 20-50 yrs. were selected for study, because this age group is 'working age group' and frequent alterations in Diet and life style or routine are observed in this age group.

4.   According to *Ayurved*, it is said to be the '*Tarunya Avastha*' of the human being which having dominance of '*Pitta Dosha*'.

➢   **Exclusion Criteria –**

1)   Patients of age group below 20 yrs. and above 50 yrs. are excluded from the study.

2)   Irregular patients not providing proper data are excluded.

3)   Patients suffering from chronic diseases such as Diabetes ,Hypertension, IHDs, Chemotherapy and Major Operative Procedures etc. are excluded.

4)   Patients suffering from signs and symptoms of *Urdhvag Amlapitta* for less than 7 days are excluded from the study.

➢   **Sampling :**

Total 100 patients within the age group 20yrs-50yrs were selected, according to simple random sampling procedure. Those were allotted into two groups:

- Group A (Trial Group) – 50 Patients.
- Group B (Control Group) – 50 Patients.

2) Selection & Preparation of drug-

Guduchi (*Tinospora cordifolia*) was selected as the Drug for the study. *Satva Kalpana* of *Guduchi* was selected for administration to the patients.

GUDUCHI

गुड़ूची-

गुड़ूची कटुकातिक्ता स्वादुपाका रसायनी ।
संग्राहिणी कषायोष्णा लघ्वी बल्याग्निदीपनी ।।
दोषत्रयाम तृड्दाहमेहकासांश्च पाण्डुताम् ।
कामला कुष्ठवातास्रज्वरक मीहरेत् ।

-(भा.प्र.नि./३/गुड़ूच्यादि वर्ग)

> **Botanical Name:** *Tinospora cordifolia*

> **Natural order:** Menispermaceae

> **Vernacular Names:**

Hindi: Giloy	**Gujarati:** Gulvel
English: Tinospora	**Marathi:** Gulvel

> **Part used:** Root, stem, leaf

> *Rasapanchaka* **(Pharmaco-dynamics):**

Rasa: Tikta, Kashaya	*Virya:* Ushna
Vipaka: Madhura	*Guna:* Guru,Snigdha

> *Doshaghnata* **:** *TriDosha Shamaka*

> **Pharmacological Activities:**

Hypoglycemic, anti-hyperglycemic, CNS depressant, antibacterial, antimicrobial, antipyretic, anti-inflammatory, analgesic, anti-arthritic, anti-allergic, hepatoprotective, immuno-stimulant, anti-neoplastic, anti-stress, antidiabetic, anti-tumor, adaptogenic, anti-leishmanial, antioxidant, antiendotoxic, hypotensive, diuretic.

➤ **Actions and Uses:**

The stem is bitter, astringent, sweet, thermogenic, anodyne, anthelminthic, antispasmodic, anti-inflammatory, antipyretic, anti-emetic, digestive, carminative, appetizer, constipating, cardiotonic, depurative, haematinic, expectorant, aphrodisiac, rejuvenating, gallacto-purifier and tonic. It is useful in **burning sensation**, hyper-dipsia, helminthiasis, **dyspepsia**, vomiting, flatulence, **acid-gastritis**, jaundice, hemorrhoids, meno-metrorrhagia, intermittent fever, tonic, inflammation, gout, cardiac debility, skin diseases, leprosy, erysipelas, anaemia, cough, asthma, general debility, seminal weakness, urinary disorders, splenomegaly, rheumatoid arthritis, fillaria, eye diseases.

The whole plant, well ground is applied on fractures. **Starch** from **roots and stem** is useful in acid diarrhea due to acidity of intestinal canal or **acid dyspepsia.**

It is useful in relieving the symptoms of rheumatism. Juice from

fresh plant is useful in diuretic. Leaves are useful in jaundice.

➤ **Substitutes and Adulterants:**

The commonest species of *Tinospora* with which *T. cordifolia* is likely to be substituted or adulterated are *T. sinesis (Lour) merr* and *T. cripsa (Linn.)*. The extract of *Guduchi (Guduchi Satva)* is adulterated with powder/flour of potato/sweet potato/arrow root/banana.

The potential offered by *T. cordifolia* against stress induced gastric mucosal damage was lost if macrophage activity was blocked.

- [Pharmacological research V. 13 (a). P (275-291) – 1999]

Preparation of '*Guduchi Satva*' for the study –

Guduchi Satva used for this study is prepared in the 'certified pharmacy' of our P.G. Institute and the certificate of standardization of the drug issued by a reputed 'Pharmacy College Lab' is attached to the Book. Whole drug manufactured under single batch number is used and product details such as manufacturing date, reference etc. are mentioned on the certificate attached in the annexure.

Preparation:

The well developed stems of the *Guduchi (Tinospora cordifolia)* were collected before rainy season. The bark of the stems was removed completely and stems were mashed. Then it was added with water, four times that of the stems and kept for 12-24 hrs. After that mashed again and filtered; and kept for settlement. The water was then removed and remaining *Satva* powder was dried well and stored properly.

(Bha.Pra.Ni./3/Guduchyadi Varga)

4.2) <u>Methods:</u>

1)   Main Aims of Study-

1) To study the *'Hetu'* of *Urdhvag Amlapitta* described in *Ayurvedic* classics.

2) To assess the importance of *Nidan Parivarjan* with administration of *Guduchi Satva.*

2)   Literature Review-

The literary source of present study was obtained from *Vedic* scriptures, classical texts of *Ayurved*, Modern texts, Published articles in reputed Journals and websites.

3)   Plan of Work for Clinical Study-

 I) Diagnostic phase.

II) Interventional Phase.

III) Assessment phase.

I)   <u>Diagnostic phase-</u>

1)   A standard case paper was prepared with routine clinical data like *Vartaman Lakshanani, Samanya Parikshan, Srotas Parikshan, Nidan Panchak* etc.

2)   The patients were diagnosed on the basis of signs and symptoms of '*Urdhvag Amlapitta*'.

3)   Patients suffering from signs and symptoms of *Urdhvag Amlapitta* for more than 7 days & within the age group of 20 yrs to 50 yrs were selected for the study.

4)   Criteria adopted for present study were as under-

A. <u>Symptoms</u> -

1. *Vanti*

2. *Shiroruja*

3. *Kara-charan Daha*

4. *Sarvang Daha*

5. *Hrid-kantha Daha*

6. *Tikta - Amla Udgar*

7. *Kandu*

8. *Aruchi*

B. <u>Signs</u> -

1. *Jvara*

2. *Mandal*

3. *Pidaka*

Aim: 1) To study the *'Hetu'* of *Urdhvag Amlapitta* described in *Ayurvedic* classics.

For assessment of *Aaharaj, Viharaj, Manasik Hetu* and those factors observed in modern life style, a suitable questionnaire in local language was provided to the diagnosed patients.

Data was obtained with the help of the questionnaire like percentage of each particular *Hetu Sevan* in all 100 patients, consumption of *Hetu* in various gradations, role of these *Hetu* in *Anshansh Samprapti* of the disease based on signs & symptoms observed.

The grading and scoring for *Hetu-sevan* was purely done on the basis of subjective information provided by the patients.

i.e.

1) *Viruddhashan* - Total 18 types are described.

0- *Asevan*

1- *Sevan* of 0-6 types / 1 time in a week.

2- *Sevan* of 7-12 types / 2-3 times in a week.

3- *Sevan* of 13-18 types / 4-7 times in a week.

2) For ***Adhyashan, Pishtanna, Apakwanna, Madyanna, Goras, Guru- Abhishyandi aahar, Atyushna, Atisnigdha, Atiruksha, Atidrava, Atiamla, Fanit-Ikshu vikar, kulattha, Bhrishta Dhanya, Pulak, Prithuk, Paryushitanna*** scoring is-

0 - *Asevan*

1 - Once in a week

2 - 2-3 times in a week

3 - 4-7 times in a week

Quantity of that particular *Hetu sevan* was decided according to subjective information only.

3) <u>*Antarodak*</u> - (Frequent ingestion of water during meals)

0 - *Asevan*

1 - Once in a meal OR few seeps.

2 - 2-3 times in a meal OR 1 glass.

3 - > 3 times OR > 1 glass of water.

4) *Divaswap* - (having sleep at day times)

 0 - *Asevan*

 1 -   1- 2 times a week OR < 1/2 hr / Day

 2 -   3- 4 times a week OR up to 1 hr / Day

 3 -   Daily OR > 1 hr / Day

5) *Bhuktwa Atisnan and Avagaha*- (Hot water bath OR Tub bath immediately after meals)

0 - *Asevan*

1 -   1 – 2 times in a week

2 -   3 – 4 times in a week

3 -   Daily

6) *Vegavidharan* - (suppression of Natural Urges due to some unavoidable situations or by habit.)

0   - *Asevan*

1   - 1-2 times a week

2   - 3-5 times a week

3   - 6-7 times a week

 7) *Aanup Desh* - (living in areas having more humidity in the air like sea shores etc.)

0   - *Asevan*

1   - Resident for 5-10 years.

2   - Resident for 10-20 years.

3   - Resident for more than 20 years.

8) *Manasik Hetu*

For *Shoka, Bhaya, Chinta*-

This scoring was done with the help of <u>DAS scale.</u>

The DASS is a set of three self-report scales designed to measure the negative emotional states of depression, anxiety and stress.

For *Krodha-*

Scoring was done on the basis of CAS i.e. Clinical Anger Scale.

Some commonly observed *Hetu* in today's lifestyle

9) Addictions -

0 - *Asevan* OR Occasionally.

1 - Consuming only supari, Pan etc. daily

2 - Tobacco, Gutakha etc daily.

3 - Intake of Alcohol, smoking, tobacco, Gutakha daily.

10) Consumption of Non-vegetarian diet, Fast food etc. -

0 - Asevan OR Occasionally.

1 - 1 - 2 times a week.

2 - 3 - 4 times a week.

3 - Daily.

11) Excess Consumption of Tea-Coffee, aerated soft drinks-

0- *Asevan* OR Occasionally.

1- 1 - 2 cups OR 1 bottle of 300 ml a day.

2- 2 - 3 cups OR 1-2 bottles of 300 ml a day.

3- > 3 cups OR > 2 bottles a day.

12) Night Duties/ Shift duties-

0   -Asevan

1   -2 to 3 days in a week

2   -4 to 5 days in a week

3   -Daily

13) Drug intake- (Like paracetamol, Ibuprofen, Diclofenac etc.NSAIDs or any other)

0   –Asevan

1   -2 to 3 days in a week

2   -4 to 5 days in a week

3   -Daily

II)   <u>Interventional Phase-</u>

Aim: 2) To assess the importance of *Nidan Parivarjan* with administration of *Guduchi Satva*.

After diagnosis of the patients, the study was intervened by the *Nidan-Parivarjan* therapy and administration of *Guduchi Satva*.

A (Trial group):	*Parivarjan + Guduchi Satva.*
B (Control group):	*i Satva* only

•   **<u>Intervention:</u>**

Group-A: Trial group

Drug   : *Guduchi Satva + Nidan Parivarjan*

Dose   : 125 mg BD

Anupana   : *Sukhoshna Jala*

Duration   : 30 days

Follow up   : once/7 days

Group-B: Control group

Drug   : *Guduchi Satva* only (Specific *Nidan Parivarjan* was not advised.)

Dose   : 125 mg BD

Anupana   : *Sukhoshna Jala*

Duration   : 30 days

Follow up   : once/7 days

- ### *Nidan Parivarjan* **Phase:**

संक्षेपतः क्रियायोगो निदानपरिवर्जनम् ।। -(सु.उ. १/२५)

Sushruta has given importance to *Nidan Parivarjan*. While explaining he defines *Nidan Parivarjan* as to leave or to avoid the causative factors. *Sushruta* further said that *Nidan Parivarjan* should be the first line of action against the disease.

According to *charaka*, though the treatment in the form of medicine is mentioned, *Nidan Parivarjan* with that medicine is beneficial for getting total relief i.e. *Apunarbhav chikitsa. Nidan Parivarjan* destroys disease from its root; hence chances of recurrence are less.

संशोधनं संशमनं निदानस्य च वर्जनम् ।
एतावद भिषजा कार्यं रोगे रोगे यथाविधि ।।
-(च.वि.)

Sanshodhana, shaman etc. kriya are of no use if *Nidan Parivarjan* is not achieved. Hence *Nidan Parivarjan* has given place, prior to *sanshodhan and shaman.*
In other words, if *Nidan Parivarjan* is achieved; then probability of getting disease is much more less than other.

In addition *Nidan Parivarjan* gives a break through in *samprapti.* If there will be no *samprapti vighatan,* then that disease will not be cured totally.

Hence, Nidan Parivarjan was advised to the patients of <u>Group A-Trial group</u>. Patients were requested to try their level best to avoid the *Hetu*; those they were consuming. If not possible completely; they were asked to reduce the frequency of *Hetu Sevan*.

<u>**III) Assessment phase-**</u>

The effects of *'Nidan-Parivarjan'* and *'Guduchi Satva'* were assessed in regards to the clinical signs and symptoms on the basis of grading and scoring systems and overall improvement; based on subjective information provided by the patients.

- **Grading and scoring -**

➢ <u>For symptoms</u> - subjective parameters were considered.

➢ <u>For signs</u> - Appropriate clinical parameters were considered.

- **Scoring**

- 0 - Normal / absence of signs & symptoms

- 1 – Mild

- 2 – Moderate

- 3- severe

- <u>**Grading & Scoring For Symptoms & Signs**</u>

<u>**A) Symptoms:**</u>

Urdhvag Amlapitta - Hetu & Nidanparivarjan   Dr. Parag Kulkarni & Dr. Amar Abhrange

1) *Vanti –*

0 - Absent

1 – 1 episode / day   OR once/wk OR less quantity

2 - 2-3 episode / day   OR 2-3 times/wk OR Moderate

3 - 3-4 episode/ day   OR > 3 times/wk OR Profuse.

2)   For *(Shiroruja, Kar-charan Daha, Sarvang Daha, Hrid-Kantha Daha, Trikta-Amla Udgar, Kandu, Aruchi)* (Subjective information)

0 - Absent

1-   Occasional - Negligible

2-   Intermittent – Not affecting routine work

3-   Continuous - Affecting routine work

4-

B) Signs:

1)   *Jvara -*

0 - Absent

1 - 99^0-100^0 F

2 - 101^0-103^0 F

3 - >103^0 F

2)   *Mandal -*

0 - Absent

1 - 1-2 mm

2 - up to 3 mm

3 - up to 5 mm

3)   *Pidaka -*

0 - Skin colour

1 - Hyperemic

2 - Red

3 - Dark Red.

<u>**Assessment:**</u>

1.	Ineffective	No effect or below 50 %
2.	Slightly effective	above 50 % up to 75 %
3.	Effective	above 75 % up to 90 %
4.	very effective	above 90 %

5) <u>Observations & Results:</u>

1) **Distribution According to sex:**

Urdhvag Amlapitta - Hetu & Nidanparivarjan Dr. Parag Kulkarni & Dr. Amar Abhrange

Group A				Group B			
S.N	Sex	No	Percentage	S.N	Sex	No	Percentage
1	Male	35	70%	1	Male	33	66%
2	Female	15	30%	2	Female	17	34%
Total		50	100%	Total		50	100%

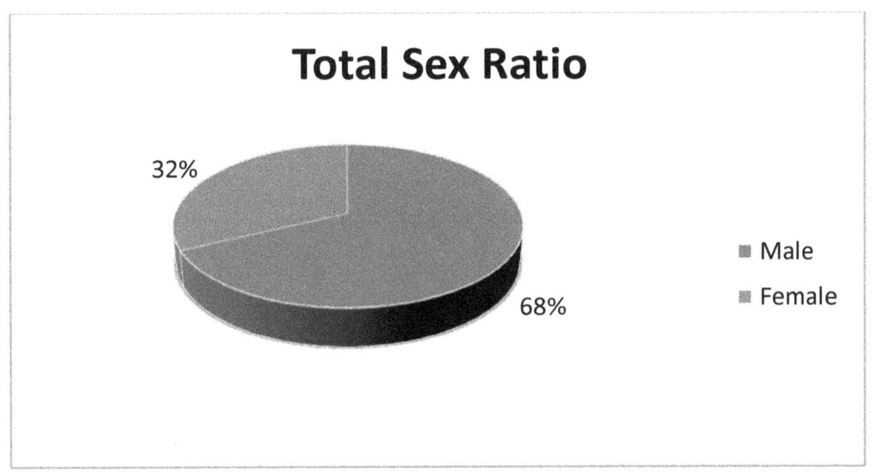

2) Distribution According to age groups:

S.N	Age	No	Percentage	S.N	Age	No	Percentage
Group A				**Group B**			
1	20-30	19	38%	1	20-30	21	42%
2	31-40	22	44%	2	31-40	23	46%
3	41-50	09	18%	3	41-50	06	12%
Total		50	100%	Total		50	100%

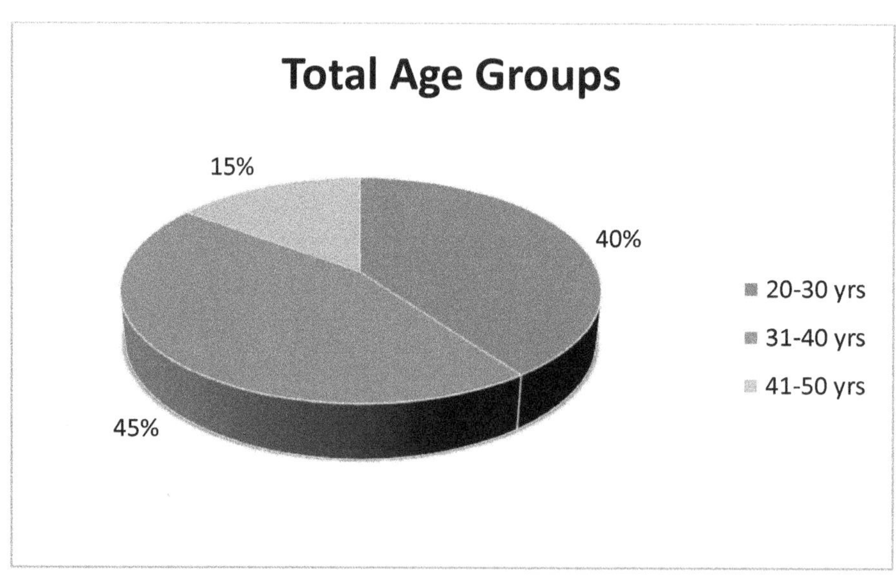

3) Distribution According to *Prakruti*:

Group A				Group B			
S.N	*Prakruti*	No	Percentage	S.N	*Prakruti*	No	Percentage
1	PK	21	42%	1	PK	23	46%
2	PV	19	38%	2	PV	16	32%
3	KV	10	20%	3	KV	11	22%
Total		50	100%	Total		50	100%

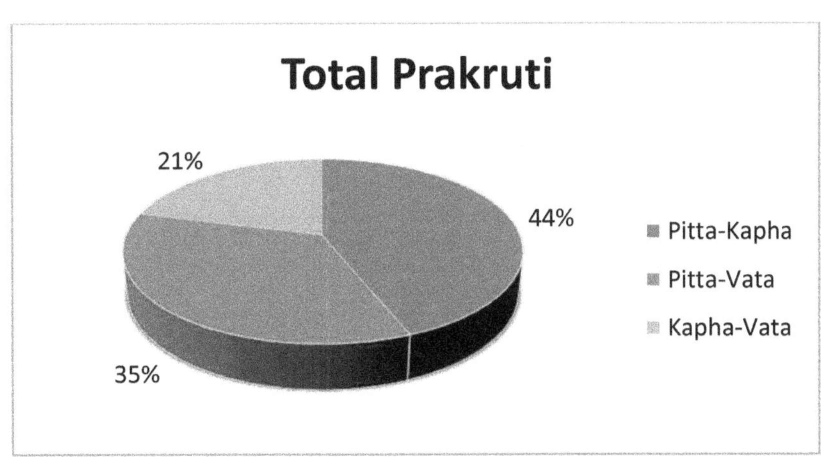

4) Distribution According to Occupations:

Group A				Group B			
S.N	**Occupation**	**No**	**Percentage**	**S.N**	**Occupation**	**No**	**Percentage**
1	Students	08	18%	1	students	10	20%
2	Housewives	11	22%	2	Housewives	11	22%
3	Farmers	12	24%	3	farmers	11	22%
4	Servicemen	12	24%	4	Servicemen	13	26%
5	Self employed	07	14%	5	Self employed	05	10%
Total		50	100%	Total		50	100%

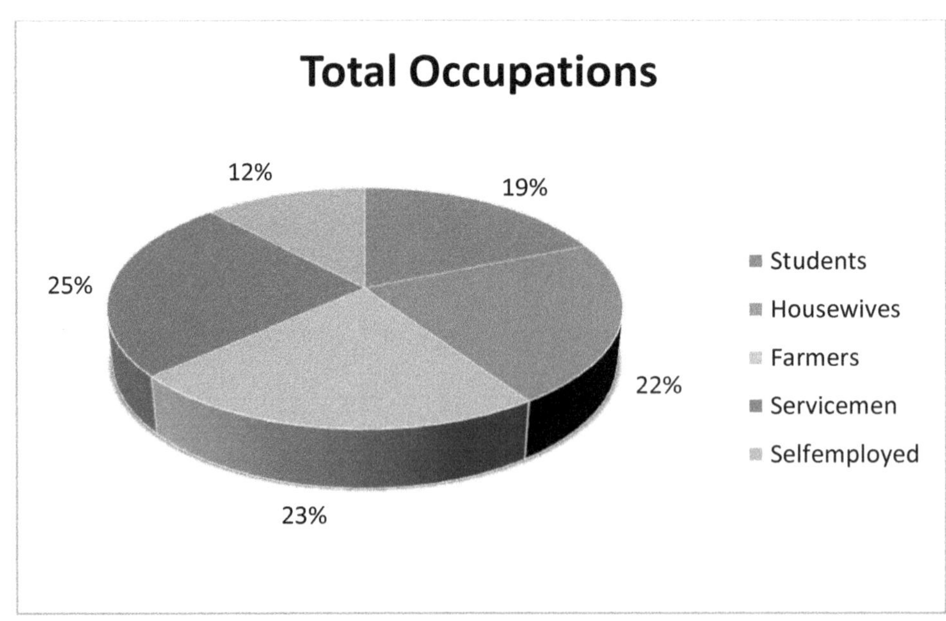

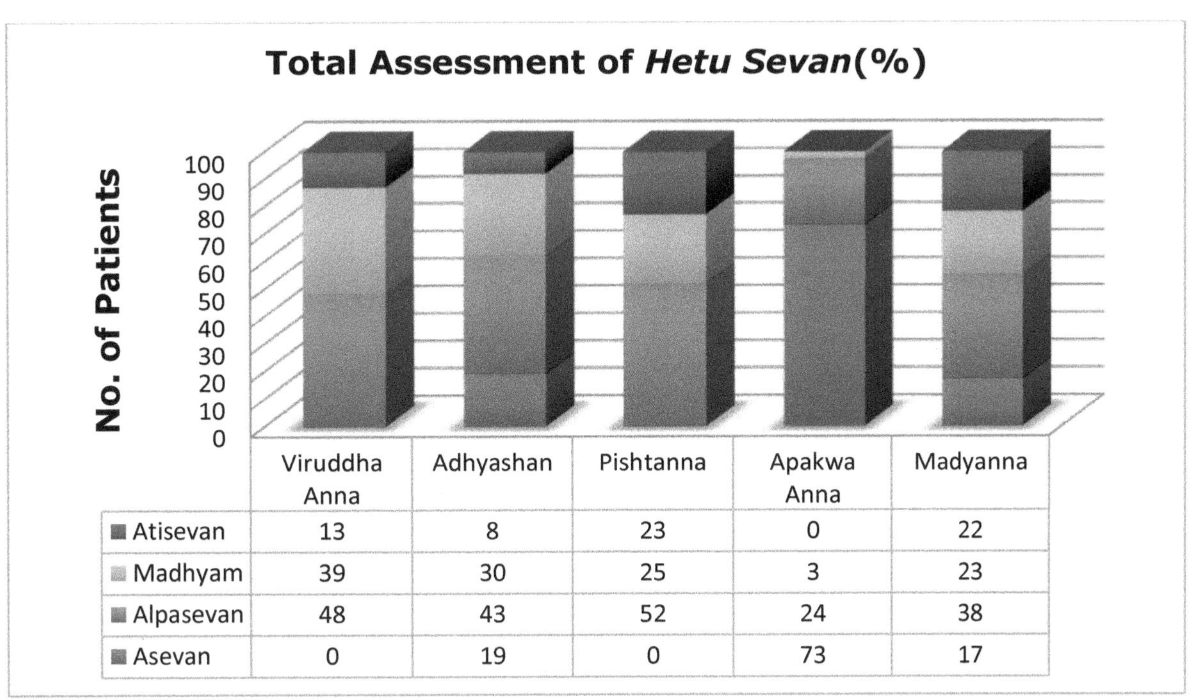

	Viruddha Anna	Adhyashan	Pishtanna	Apakwa Anna	Madyanna
▪ Atisevan	13	8	23	0	22
▪ Madhyam	39	30	25	3	23
▪ Alpasevan	48	43	52	24	38
▪ Asevan	0	19	0	73	17

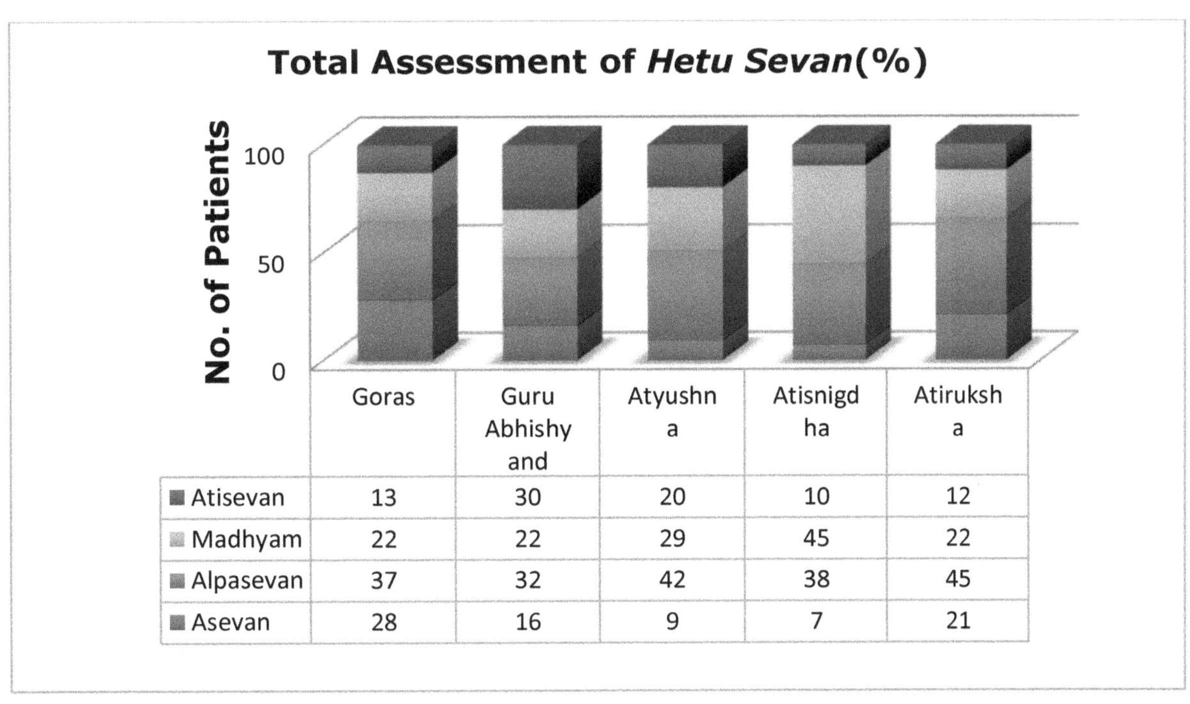

	Goras	Guru Abhishy and	Atyushna	Atisnigdha	Atiruksha
▪ Atisevan	13	30	20	10	12
▪ Madhyam	22	22	29	45	22
▪ Alpasevan	37	32	42	38	45
▪ Asevan	28	16	9	7	21

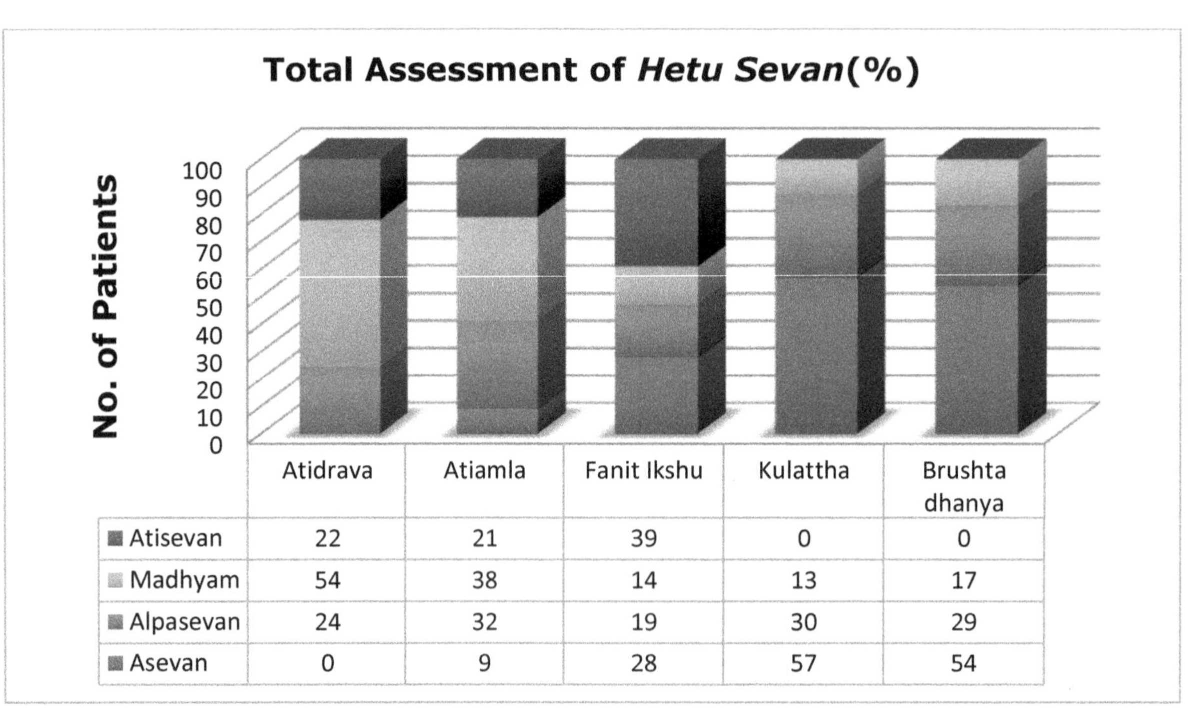

Total Assessment of *Hetu Sevan*(%)

	Atidrava	Atiamla	Fanit Ikshu	Kulattha	Brushta dhanya
Atisevan	22	21	39	0	0
Madhyam	54	38	14	13	17
Alpasevan	24	32	19	30	29
Asevan	0	9	28	57	54

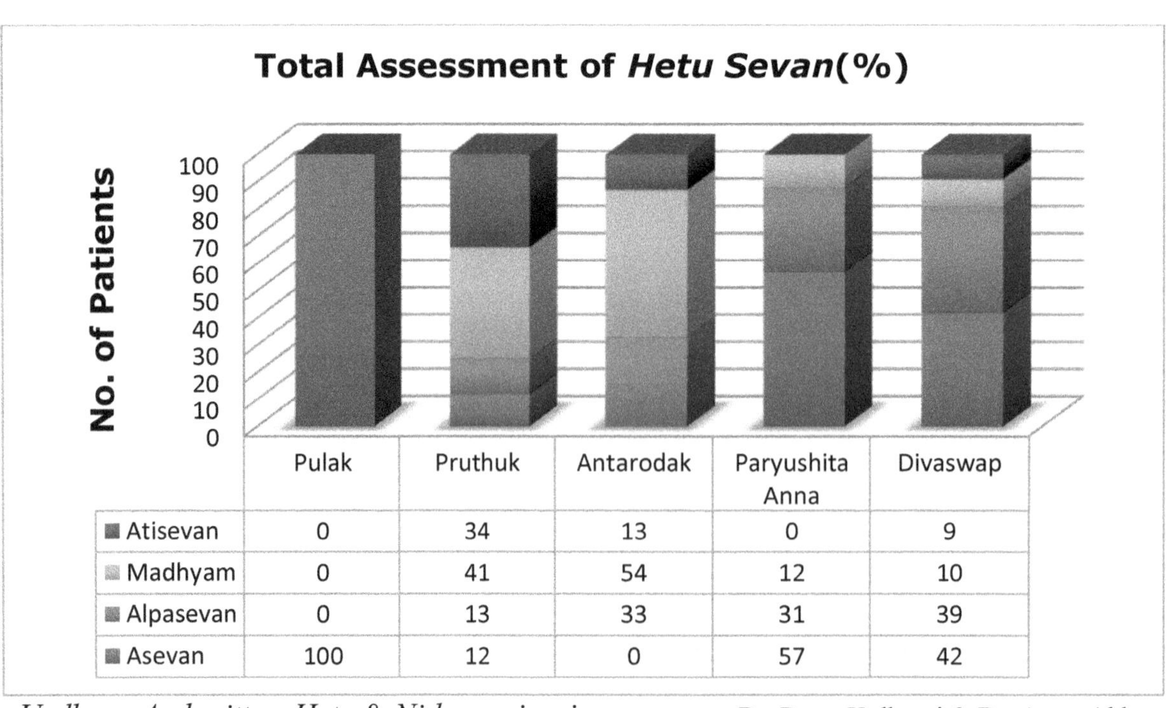

Total Assessment of *Hetu Sevan*(%)

	Pulak	Pruthuk	Antarodak	Paryushita Anna	Divaswap
Atisevan	0	34	13	0	9
Madhyam	0	41	54	12	10
Alpasevan	0	13	33	31	39
Asevan	100	12	0	57	42

Total Assessment of *Hetu Sevan*(%)

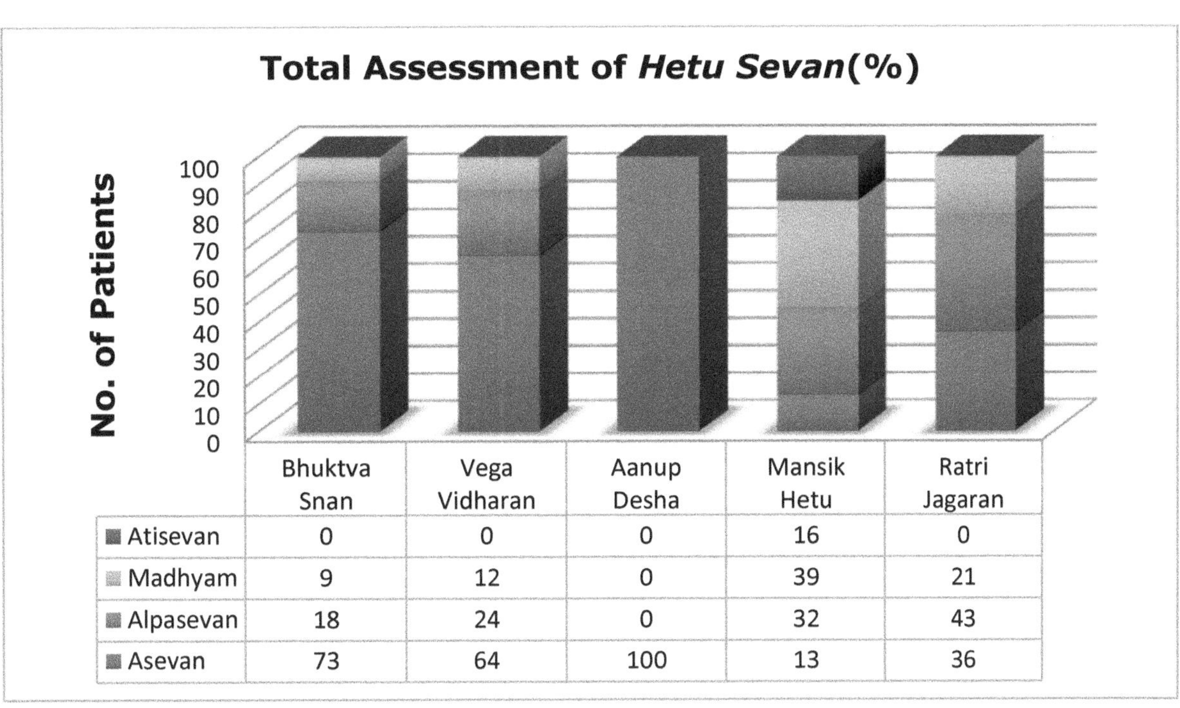

	Bhuktva Snan	Vega Vidharan	Aanup Desha	Mansik Hetu	Ratri Jagaran
Atisevan	0	0	0	16	0
Madhyam	9	12	0	39	21
Alpasevan	18	24	0	32	43
Asevan	73	64	100	13	36

Total Assessment of *Hetu Sevan*(%)

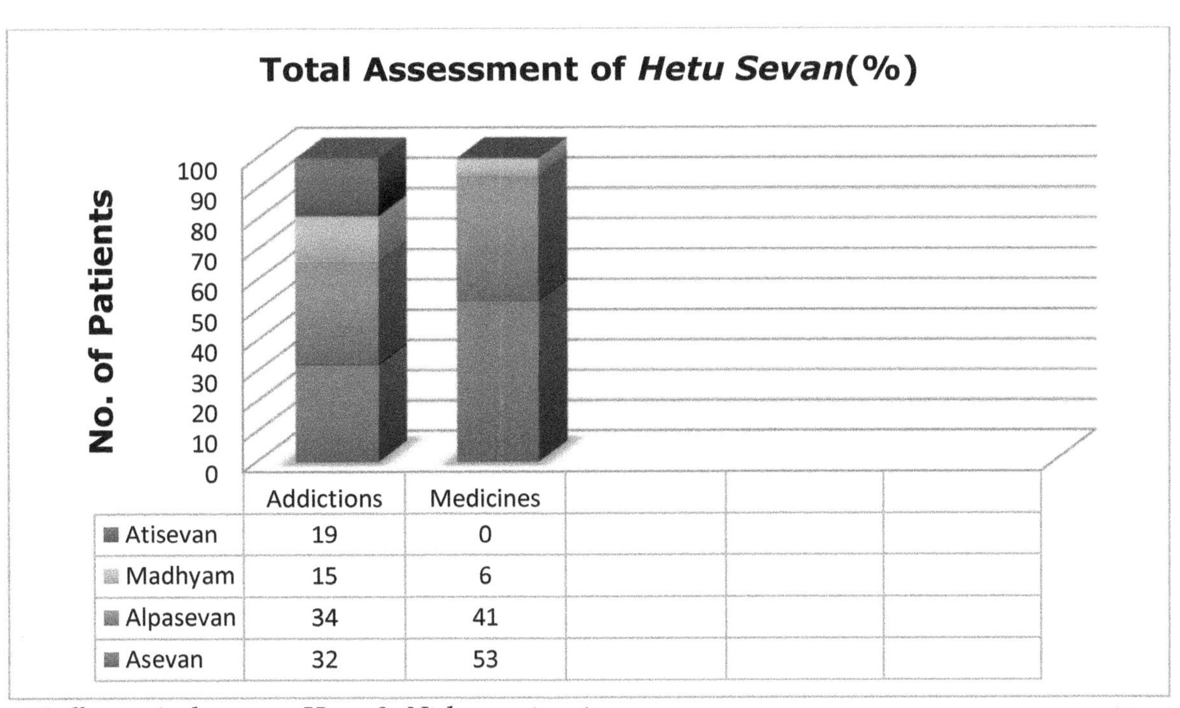

	Addictions	Medicines
Atisevan	19	0
Madhyam	15	6
Alpasevan	34	41
Asevan	32	53

No.	Symptom/Sign	Group A	Group B	Total (%)
1.	*Vanti*	43	41	84
2.	*Shiroruja*	44	42	86
3.	*Tikta-Amla Udgar*	46	45	91
4.	*Hrid-Kantha Daha*	42	40	82
5.	*Kara-Charan Daha*	29	26	55
6.	*Sarvanga Daha*	23	21	44
7.	*Aruchi*	21	18	39
8.	*Kandu*	12	14	26
9.	*Jvara*	03	04	07
10.	*Mandal*	00	00	00
11.	*Pidaka*	00	00	00

- **<u>General Features of the disease observed in the study:</u>**

Follow-Up Day	GROUP	CURED	UNCURED	x^2 Value at 0.05 L. Of S. , D.F.-1	x^2 value in table	Inference p
7th day I FU	A	20	23	0.8508	3.84	Insignificant p>0.05
	B	15	26			
14th day II FU	A	26	17	3.03	3.84	Insignificant p>0.05
	B	17	24			
21st day II FU	A	32	11	4.8510	3.84	Significant P<0.05
	B	21	20			
28th day IV FU	A	38	05	1.6104	3.84	Insignificant p>0.05
	B	32	09			

- ## **Disease relief charts (Signs & symptoms)**

1) *Vanti:*

Follow-Up Day	GROUP	CURED	UNCURED	x^2 Value at 0.05 L. Of S. , D.F.-1	x^2 value in table	Inference p
7th day I FU	A	06	38	0.3536	3.84	Insignificant p>0.05
	B	04	38			
14th day II FU	A	10	34	1.7478	3.84	Insignificant p>0.05
	B	05	37			
21st day III FU	A	23	21	6.1151	3.84	Significant p<0.05
	B	11	31			
28th day IV FU	A	35	09	8.2579	3.84	Significant p<0.05
	B	21	21			

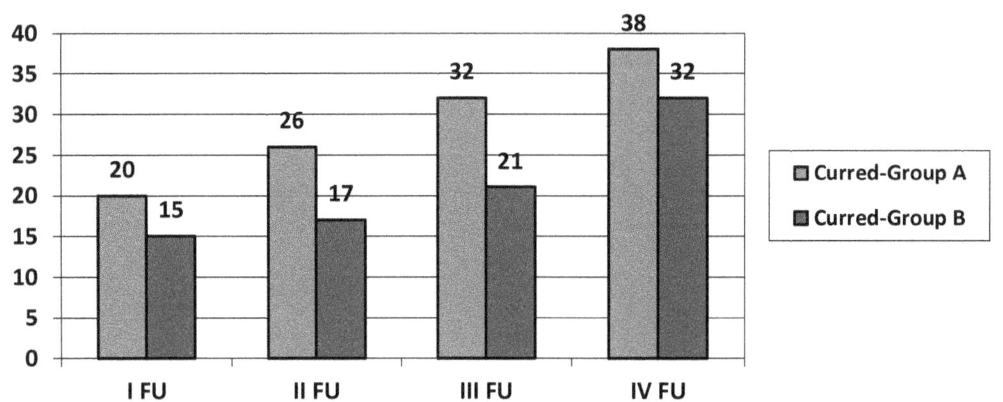

2) *Shiroruja:*

Follow-Up Day	GROUP	CURED	UNCURED	x^2 Value at 0.05 L. Of S. , D.F.-1	x^2 value in table	Inference p
7th day I FU	A	06	38	0.3536	3.84	Insignificant p>0.05
	B	04	38			
14th day II FU	A	10	34	1.7478	3.84	Insignificant p>0.05
	B	05	37			
21st day III FU	A	23	21	6.1151	3.84	Significant p<0.05
	B	11	31			
28th day IV FU	A	35	09	8.2579	3.84	Significant p<0.05
	B	21	21			

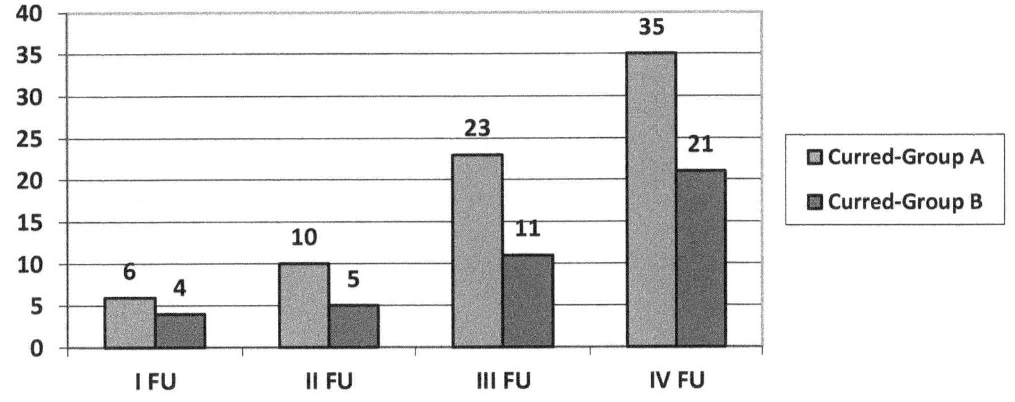

3) Tikta-Amla Udgar:

Urdhvag Amlapitta - Hetu & Nidanparivarjan   Dr. Parag Kulkarni & Dr. Amar Abhrange

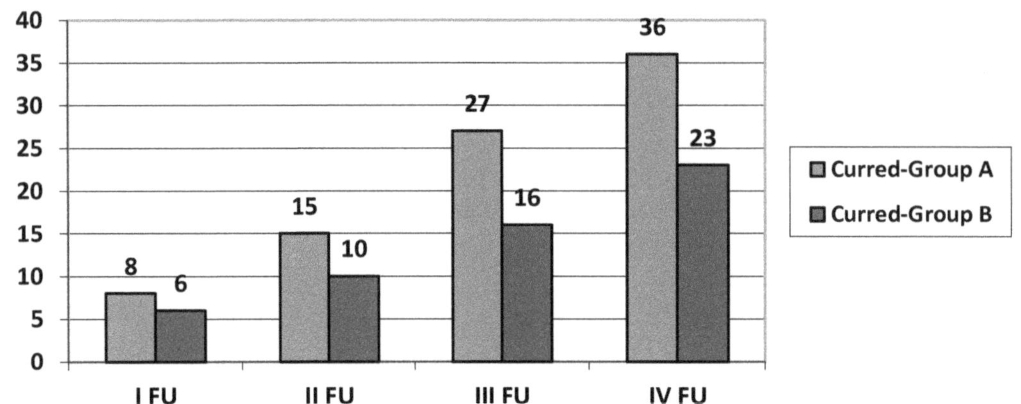

4) Hrid-Kantha Daha:

Follow-Up Day	GROUP	CURED	UNCURED	x^2 Value at 0.05 L. Of S. , D.F.-1	x^2 value in table	Inference p
7th day I FU	A	12	30	1.41	3.84	Insignificant p>0.05
	B	07	33			
14th day II FU	A	20	22	3.5270	3.84	Insignificant p>0.05
	B	11	29			
21st day III FU	A	29	13	5.8629	3.84	Significant p<0.05
	B	17	23			
28th day IV FU	A	38	04	9.0075	3.84	Significant p<0.05
	B	25	15			

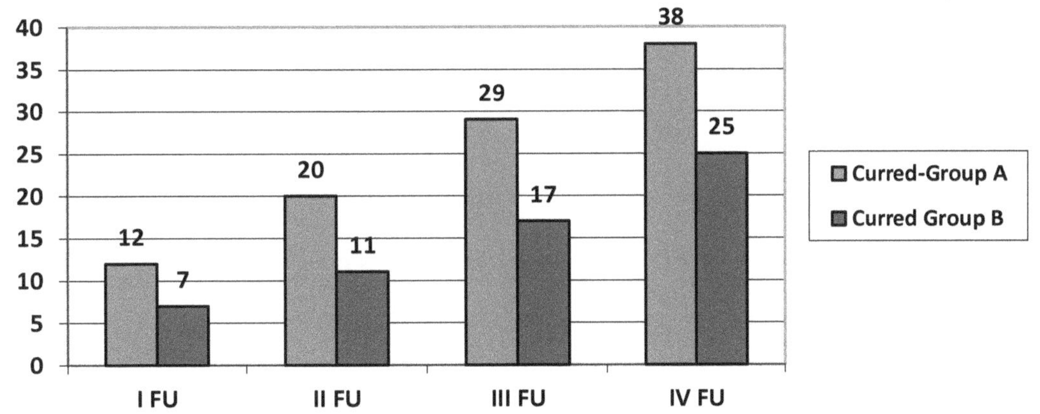

5) *Kara-Charan Daha:*

Follow-Up Day	GROUP	CURED	UNCURED	x^2 Value at 0.05 L. Of S. , D.F.-1	x^2 value in table	Inference p
7th day I FU	A	11	18	1.4164	3.84	Insignificant p>0.05
	B	06	20			
14th day II FU	A	15	14	2.4741	3.84	Insignificant p>0.05
	B	08	18			
21st day III FU	A	22	07	7.88	3.84	Significant p<0.05
	B	10	16			
28th day IV FU	A	25	04	9.98	3.84	Significant p<0.05
	B	12	14			

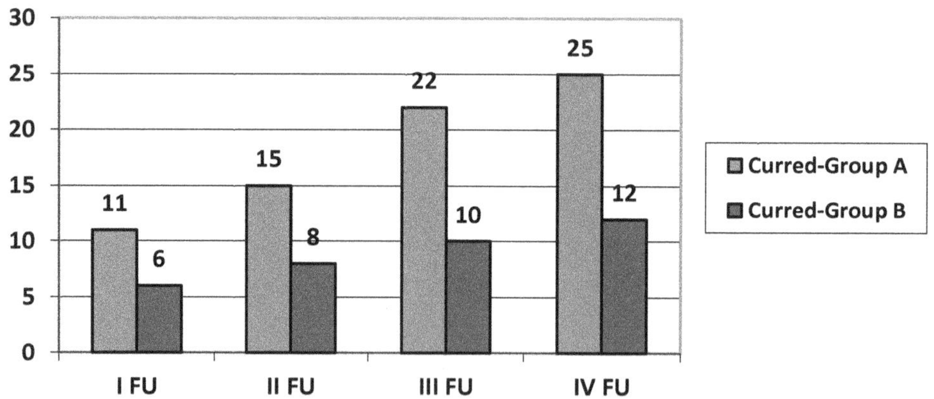

6) *Sarvanga Daha:*

Follow-Up Day	GROUP	CURED	UNCURED	x^2 Value at 0.05 L. Of S. , D.F.-1	x^2 value in table	Inference p
7th day I FU	A	06	17	0.0303	3.84	Insignificant p>0.05
	B	05	16			
14th day II FU	A	13	10	2.3806	3.84	Insignificant p>0.05
	B	07	14			
21st day III FU	A	19	04	4.6234	3.84	Significant p<0.05
	B	11	10			
28th day IV FU	A	23	00	7.6090	3.84	Significant p<0.05
	B	15	06			

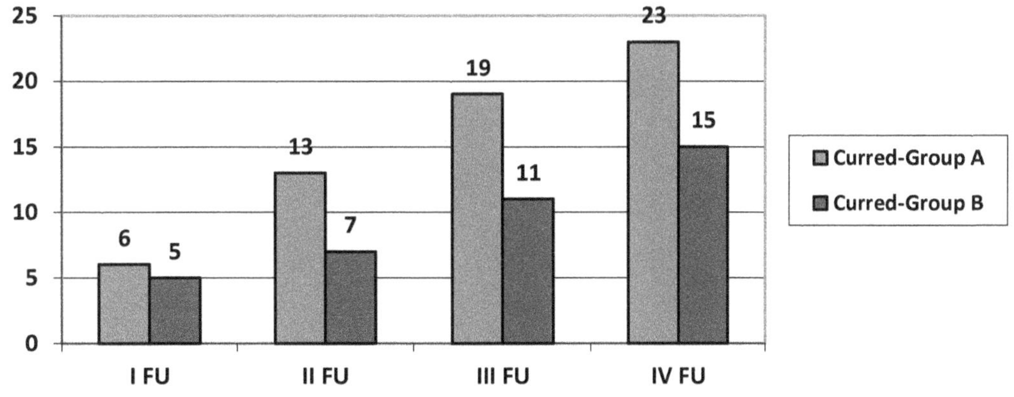

7) *Aruchi:*

Urdhvag Amlapitta - Hetu & Nidanparivarjan   Dr. Parag Kulkarni & Dr. Amar Abhrange

Follow-Up Day	GROUP	CURED	UNCURED	x^2 Value at 0.05 L. Of S. , D.F.-1	x^2 value in table	Inference p
7th day I FU	A	09	11	1.2076	3.84	Insignificant p>0.05
	B	05	13			
14th day II FU	A	13	08	2.0550	3.84	Insignificant p>0.05
	B	07	11			
21st day III FU	A	17	04	4.1785	3.84	Significant p<0.05
	B	09	09			
28th day IV FU	A	20	01	3.9440	3.84	Significant p<0.05
	B	13	05			

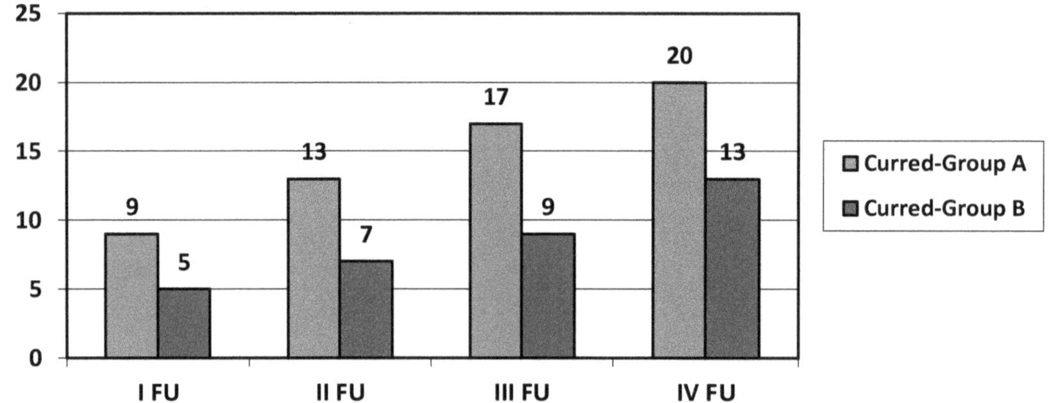

8) *Kandu:*

Follow-Up Day	GROUP	CURED	UNCURED	x^2 Value at 0.05 L. Of S. , D.F.-1	x^2 value in table	Inference p
7th day I FU	A	04	08	0.4654	3.84	Insignificant p>0.05
	B	03	11			
14th day II FU	A	07	05	1.3302	3.84	Insignificant p>0.05
	B	05	09			
21st day III FU	A	10	02	4.4726	3.84	Significant p<0.05
	B	06	08			
28th day IV FU	A	12	00	2.9068	3.84	Insignificant p>0.05
	B	11	03			

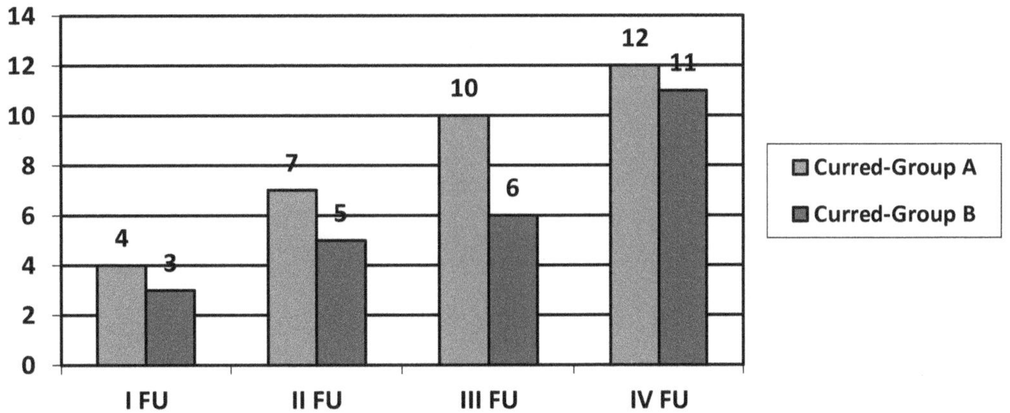

9) *Jvara:*

Number of patients having the symptom '*Jvara*' in both the groups is:

Urdhvag Amlapitta - Hetu & Nidanparivarjan   Dr. Parag Kulkarni & Dr. Amar Abhrange

Group A: 03

Group B: 04

These numbers are very less; hence these are inadequate for statistical analysis by applying statistical tests like CHI^2 test.

That is why it is not practically possible to draw any inference from these numbers.

10) *Mandal* & 11) *Pidaka :*

These two signs were totally absent in all patients from both the groups. Hence there is no chance of statistical analysis and inference.

- **<u>Overall relief in clinical features of *Urdhvag Amlapitta*</u>:**

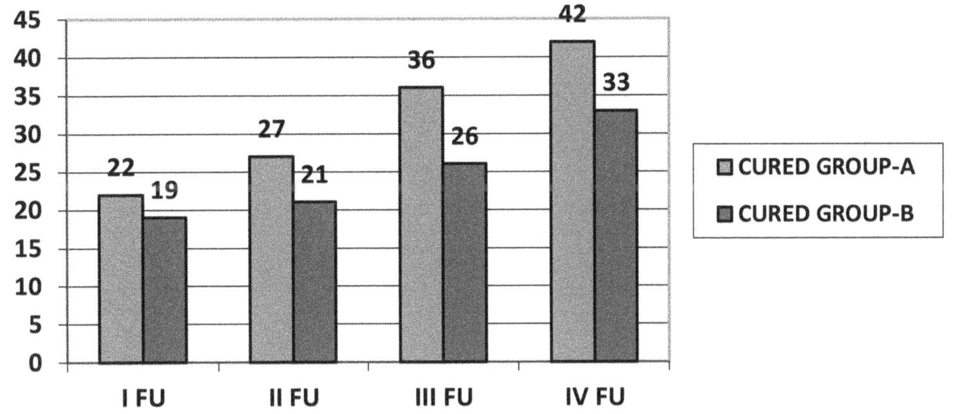

6) <u>Discussion:</u>

The main aim of *Ayurved* is to maintain the health of the healthy person and to cure the illness of the diseased person. It is capable of dealing with problems related with modern life-style.

Present book uncovers one of such burning problems i.e. *'Urdhvag AmplaPitta'*. This work is mainly concentrated on certain prominent *'Hetu'* which are described in our *Ayurvedic* texts under various categories like *Aaharaj Hetu, Viharaj Hetu, Manasik Hetu* etc. Moreover nowadays people do not follow the rules like *'Dincharya'* and *'Ritucharya'*. All these things disturb the balance of *'TriDosha'*.

It will be helpful for us to avoid such kind of *Hetu* (i.e. *Nidan-parivarjan*) and remain safe, unaffected from such a serious problem.

Hence, an attempt is made to understand these *Hetu & Nidan Parivarjan* of *Urdhvag Amlapitta* in this book titled- *"URDHVAG AMLAPITTA – HETU & NIDAN PARIVARJAN"*

For the research, 100 individuals were studied in two groups. i.e. 50 individuals in each group having age between 20 yrs to 50 yrs as mentioned in material and methods.

2)   Distribution According to sex in total 100 patients:

- Male: 68%

- Female: 32%

Males are more affected by *Urdhvag Amlapitta.* Life style, particular *Hetu Sevan*, working patterns, irregular dietary habits, stress and addictions etc. factors may be responsible for this and should be studied in detail. *Nidan Parivarjan* must be advised compulsorily to them.

3)   Distribution According to age groups in total 100 patients:

- Patients in age group 20 yrs to 30 yrs are: 40%

- Patients in age group 31 yrs to 40 yrs are: 45%

- Patients in age group 41 yrs to 50 yrs are: 15%

Here, people in age group 31 yrs to 40 yrs are likely more prone to *Urdhvag Amlapitta.* Even percentage in age group 20 yrs to 30 yrs is also not too less. These groups are engaged in academic activities, jobs, bussy physical & mental activities. According to *Ayurved* it is peak level of *'Tarunyavastha'* & *'Pitta Dosh'* dominance; hence large scale study should be concentrated on these age groups.

4)   **Distribution According to *Prakruti* in total 100 patients**:

- Patients having *Pitta-Kapha Prakruti* are: 44%

- Patients having *Pitta-Vata Prakruti* are: 35%

- Patients having *Kapha-Vata Prakruti* are: 21%

- Patients having *Ek-Doshaj* & *Tri-Doshaj Prakruti* were not found.

Here, prevalence of the disease in *Pitta-Kapha Prakruti* is more than any other *Prakruti*.

5)   **Distribution According to Occupations in total 100 patients :**

- Patients having occupation- 'Students' are: 18%

- Patients having occupation- 'Housewives' are: 22%

- Patients having occupation- 'Farmers' are: 23%

- Patients having occupation- 'servicemen' are: 25%

- Patients having occupation- 'Self-employed/Business' are: 12%

Here, people in working class or service class are more sufferers than any other occupations. This may be because of irregular dietary habits, long working hours, more traveling and severe competition etc. factors restrict or divert these individuals from proper 'Dinacharyapalan' & 'Rutucharyapalan'.

<u>**Distribution of total 100 patients on the basis of particular *'Hetu Sevan'*:**</u>

Grade 0- *Asevan*

Grade 1- *Alpasevan*

Grade 2- *Madhyamsevan*   total 100% for each *'Hetu'*.

Grade 3- *Atisevan*

1) *Viruddhashan:*

0-   *Asevan* = 0%

1-   *Sevan* of 0-6 types / 1 time in a week = 48%

2-   *Sevan* of 7-12 types / 2-3 times in a week = 39%

3-   *Sevan* of 13-18 types / 4-7 times in a week = 13%

People in *'Alpasevan'* category are more in this *Hetu.*

2) *Adhyashan:*

0 - *Asevan* = 19%

1 - Once in a week = 43%

2 - 2-3 times in a week = 30%

3 - 4-7 times in a week = 8%

Number of patients in *'Alpasevan'* group is comparatively large.

3) *Pishtanna:*

0 - *Asevan* = 0%

1 - Once in a week = 52%

2 - 2-3 times in a week = 25%

3 - 4-7 times in a week = 23%

'Alpasevan' category is having more number of patients.

4) *Apakwanna:*

0 - *Asevan* = 73%

1 - Once in a week = 24%

2 - 2-3 times in a week = 3%

3 - 4-7 times in a week = 0%

People in *'Asevan'* category are more in this *Hetu.*

5) *Madyanna:*

0 - *Asevan* = 17%

1 - Once in a week = 38%

2 - 2-3 times in a week = 23%

3 - 4-7 times in a week = 22%

Number of patients in '*Alpasevan*' group is comparatively large.

6) *Goras:*

0 - *Asevan* = 28%

1 - Once in a week = 37%

2 - 2-3 times in a week = 22%

3 - 4-7 times in a week = 13%

'*Alpasevan*' category is having more number of patients.

7) *Guru- Abhishyandi aahar:*

0 - *Asevan* = *16%*

1 - Once in a week = 32%

2 - 2-3 times in a week = 22%

3 - 4-7 times in a week = 30%

More number of patients have consumed this *Hetu* in '*Alpasevan Matra*'.

8) *Atyushna:*

0 - *Asevan* = *9%*

1 - Once in a week = 42%

2 - 2-3 times in a week = 29%

3 - 4-7 times in a week = 20%

People in '*Asevan*' category are more in this *Hetu.*

9) *Atisnigdha:*

0 - *Asevan* = *7%*

1 - Once in a week = 38%

2   - 2-3 times in a week = 45%

3   - 4-7 times in a week = 10%

'*Madhyamsevan*' category is having more number of patients.

10)   *Atiruksha:*

0 -*Asevan = 11%*

1 -Once in a week = 35%

2- 2-3 times in a week = 42%

3- 4-7 times in a week = 12%

More number of patients have consumed this *Hetu* in *'Madhyamsevan Matra.'*

11)   *Atidrava:*

0 - *Asevan = 0%*

1 - Once in a week = 24%

2 - 2-3 times in a week = 54%

3 - 4-7 times in a week = 22%

Number of patients in *'Madhyamsevan'* group is comparatively large.

12)   *Atiamla:*

0 - *Asevan = 9%*

1 - Once in a week = 32%

2 - 2-3 times in a week = 38%

3 - 4-7 times in a week = 21%

 People in *'Madhyamsevan'* category are more in this *Hetu.*

13)   *Fanit-Ikshu vikar:*

0 – *Asevan* = 28%

1 - Once in a week = 19%

2 - 2-3 times in a week = 14%

3- 4-7 times in a week = 39%

More number of patients have consumed this *Hetu* in 'Atisevan   Matra'.

14)   *Kulattha:*

0 - *Asevan* = 57%

1 - Once in a week = 30%

2 - 2-3 times in a week = 13%

3 - 4-7 times in a week = 0%

 'Asevan' category is having more number of patients.

15) *Bhrishta Dhanya:*

0 - *Asevan* = 54%

1 - Once in a week = 29%

2 - 2-3 times in a week = 17%

3 - 4-7 times in a week = 0%

More number of patients have consumed this *Hetu* in '*Asevan   Matra.*'

16) *Pulak:*

0 - *Asevan* = 100%

1 - Once in a week = 0%

2 - 2-3 times in a week = 0%

3 - 4-7 times in a week = 0%

Here, people consuming 'Pulak' were not found in the study.

17) *Prithuk:*

0 - *Asevan* = 12%

1 - Once in a week = 13%

2 - 2-3 times in a week = 41%

3 - 4-7 times in a week = 34%

People in '*Madhyamsevan*' category are more in this *Hetu.*

18) *Paryushitanna:*

0 - *Asevan* = 57%

1 - Once in a week = 31%

2 - 2-3 times in a week = 12%

3 - 4-7 times in a week = 0%

People in '*Asevan*' category are more in this *Hetu.*

19) *Antarodak* - (Frequent ingestion of water during meals)

0 – *Asevan* = 0 %

1 - Once in a meal OR few seeps = 33%

2 - 2-3 times in a meal OR 1 glass = 54%

3 - > 3 times OR > 1 glass of water = 13%

Number of patients in '*Madhyamsevan*' group is comparatively large.

20) *Divaswap* - (having sleep at day times)

0 - *Asevan* = 42%

1 - 1-2 times a week OR < 1/2 hr / Day = 39%

2 - 3-4 times a week OR up to 1 hr / Day = 10%

3 - Daily OR > 1 hr / Day = 9%

'*Asevan*' category is having more number of patients.

21) ***Bhuktwa Atisnan and Avagaha***- (Hot water bath OR Tub bath immediately after meals)

0 - *Asevan* = 73%

1 - 1 – 2 times in a week = 18%

2 - 3 – 4 times in a week = 9%

3 - Daily = 0%

People in '*Asevan*' category are more in this *Hetu.*

22) ***Vegavidharan*** - (suppression of Natural Urges due to some unavoidable situations or by habit.)

0 -*Asevan* = 64%

1 - 1-2 times a week = 24%

2- 3-5 times a week = 12%

3-6-7 times a week = 0%

People in '*Asevan*' category are more in this *Hetu.*

23) ***Aanup Desh*** - (living in areas having more humidity in the air like sea shores etc.)

0- *Asevan* = *100%*

1 - Resident for 5-10 years = 0%

2- Resident for 10-20 years = 0%

3- Resident for more than 20 years = 0%

Patients from *Aanup Desh* did not approach to the OPDs.

24) ***Manasik Hetu:***   (*Krodha, Shoka, Bhaya, Chinta* etc.)

Grade 0 - *Asevan* = 13%

Grade 1 - *Alpasevan* = 32%

Grade 2 - *Atisevan* = 39%

Grade 3 - *Madhyamsevan* = 16%

More number of people were affected by *Mansik Hetu* in grade 2.

25)   Addictions -

0 - *Asevan* OR Occasionally = 32%

1 - Consuming only supari, Pan etc. daily = 34%

2 - Tobacco, Gutakha etc daily = 15%

3- Intake of Alcohol, smoking, tobacco, Gutakha daily = 19%

People in '*Alpasevan*' category are more in this *Hetu.*

26)   Night Duties/ Shift duties- (*Ratri-Jagaran*)

0-*Asevan* = 36%

1- 2 to 3 days in a week = 43%

2- 4 to 5 days in a week = 21%

3- Daily = 0%

Number of patients in '*Alpasevan*' group is comparatively large.

27)   Drug intake- (Like paracetamol, Ibuprofen, Diclofenac etc.NSAIDs or any other)

4   – *Asevan* = 53%

5   - 2 to 3 days in a week = 41%

6   - 4 to 5 days in a week = 6%

7   - Daily = 0%

People in '*Asevan*' category are more in this *Hetu.*

<u>Co-relation of some newly found *Hetu* with classical *Ayurvedic Hetu* mentioned in texts</u>

	Newly found *Hetu*	**classical *Ayurvedic Hetu***
1.	Non vegetarian diet, fast food	*~Guru-Abhishyandi aahar*
2.	Excess Consumption of Tea, Coffee, aerated soft drinks	*~Atidrava*
3.	Addictions	*~Madyanna/Atyushna*
4.	Drug intake	*~Atyushna*
5.	Night duties (*Ratri-Jagaran*)	*~Atiruksha*

According to above co-relation, some of these modern life *'Hetu'* are included in to their respective *'Ayurvedic Hetu'* category and scoring pattern is applied to them instead of presenting their separate entity.

It can be assumed that these new *'Hetu'* have acted similarly to their respective *Ayurvedic Hetu* in general *Samprapti* as well as *Anshansh Samprapti* of the disease.

<u>*Anshansh Samprapti:*</u>

Probable Relationship inbetween Signs-Symptoms and *Pitta Guna*

पित्तं सस्नेहं तीक्ष्णोष्णं लघु विस्रं सरं द्रवं । -(अ.सं.सू.१)

	Snigdha	*Tikshna*	*Ushna*	*Laghu*	*Vistra*	*sara*	*Drava*
Vanti					+	+	+
Shiroruja		+		+			
Kara-Charan Daha		+	+	+			
Sarvang Daha		+	+	+			
Hrid-Kantha Daha		+	+				+
Tikta-Amla Udgar					+	+	+
Kandu	+		+				+
Aruchi	+					+	+
Jvara		+	+				
Mandal	+		+				
Pidaka		+	+	+			

Relationship observed in between *Granthokta Hetu-Sevan* & *Pitta Guna* & Occurred *Urdhvag Amlapitta Lakshana*:

	Hetu Sevan	Pitta Guna Vruddhi	Lakshana
1	*Virudhdhh Anna*	*Snigdha,tikshna,ushna, visra ,sara, drava*	*Vanti,shiroruja, daha, udgar, aruchi*
2	*Adhyashana*	*Snigdha,sara,drava*	*Vanti,aruchi*
3	*Pishtanna*	*Snigdha,visra,sara*	*Aruchi*
4	*Apakwanna*	*Snigdha,visra,drava*	*Vanti,aruchi*
5	*Madyanna*	*Ushna,tikshna,sara,drava*	*Vanti,daha,udgar*
6	*Goras*	*Snigdha,drava,sara*	*Vanti,aruchi,kandu*
7	*Guru-Abhishyandi*	*Snigdha,sara,visra*	*Aruchi,kandu,vanti*
8	*Atyushna*	*Ushna,tikshna,laghu,*	*Daha,udgar,jvara*
9	*Ati-Snigdha*	*Snigdha,visra,drava,sara*	*Aruchi,kandu,vanti*
10	*Ati-Ruksha*	*Laghu,tikshna*	*Shiroruja,aruchi,vanti*
11	*Dravanam*	*Drava,sara,visra,snigdha*	*Vanti,aruchi,udgar, kandu*
12	*Ati-Amla*	*Ushna,tikshna,drava*	*Vanti,daha,udgar*
13	*Fanit-Ikshu Vikar*	*Drava,sara,snigdha,visra*	*Vanti,aruchi,kandu*
14	*Kulattha*	*Tikshna,laghu,ushna*	*Shiroruja,daha,udgar*
15	*Brushta Dhanya*	*Laghu,tikshna,ushna*	*Daha,udgar,shiroruja*
16	*Pulak (Asevan)*	Sample Not Found	Sample Not Found
17	*Pruthuk*	*Ushna,tikshna,visra*	*Daha,udgar,vanti*
18	*Antarodak*	*Drava,sara,snigdha*	*Vanti,aruchi,udgar*
19	*Paryushitanna*	*Visra,tikshna,ushna*	*Vanti,aruchi,shiroruja, daha,udgar*
20	*Divaswap*	*Snigdha*	*Aruchi,kandu,shiroruja*
21	*Bhuktva Snan*	*Ushna,drava,snigdha*	*Vanti,daha,udgar*
22	*Vega Vidharan*	*Laghu,visra,tikshna,ushna*	*Shiroruja,aruchi,udgar*
23	*Aanup Desha(Asevan)*	Sample Not Found	Sample Not Found

- *Daha = Hrid-Kantha, Kara-Charan, Sarvang Daha.*

- *Udgar = Tikta-Amla Udgar.*

With reference to previous presented chart, we can explain the *Anshansha Samprapti* of *Urdhvag Amlapitta* in a general format as below. Particular *Hetu Sevan* will aggravate particular *Pitta Guna* and *Dosh-Dushya Samurchchhana* takes place; and accordingly signs-symptoms occur.

Schematic presentation of Anshansha *Samprapti* of *Amlapitta*

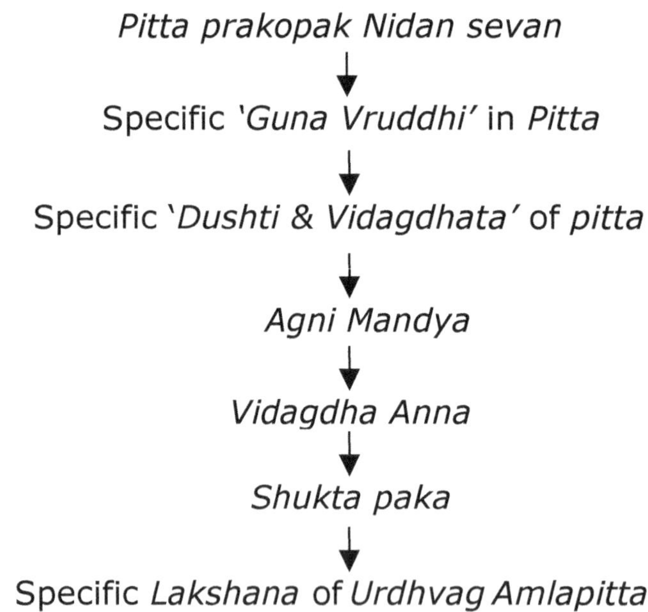

Role of *Nidan Parivarjan* in *Samprapti Vighatan*:

If these specific *Hetu* causing Specific *Guna Vriddhi* of *Pitta Dosha* are avoided or their intake is reduced; then ultimately vitiation or Aggravation of *Pitta Dosha* by that particular *Guna* will not take place.

This will lead to break the *Samprapti* & further disease will not be formed. Hence, *Nidan Parivarjan* is important to prevent the disease from its initial and preliminary stage.

"Prevention is better than Cure!"

Various Clinical Features of the disease observed in the study:

Among all clinical features of the *Urdhvag Amlapitta*; *Tikta-Amlodgar, Shiroruja, Vanti, Hrid-Kantha Daha* were the major symptoms. Patients suffering from- Tikta-Amlodgar were

91%, Shiroruja were 86%, Vanti were 84% and *Hrid-Kantha Daha* were 82%. Hence these can be considered as the major Cardinal Symptoms of the disease.

Kara-Charan Daha was 55%, *Sarvang Daha* was 44%, *Aruchi* was 39%, *kandu* was 26% and *Jvara* was only 07%. These were comparatively less seen features.

Signs like *Mandal* and *Pidaka* were totally absent in observed patients indicating that these might be rare features or occurring in severe, advanced and chronic stages of the disease.

- ### **Symptomatic relief of the disease in the Interventional Phase:**

After diagnosis of the patients, the study was intervened by the *Nidan-Parivarjan* therapy and administration of *Guduchi Satva.*

Group A (Trial group):	*Nidan Parivarjan + Guduchi Satva.*
Group B (Control group):	*Guduchi Satva* only

Following criteria were adopted to assess the results obtained in all signs & symptoms-

1.	Ineffective	No effect or below 50 %
2.	Slightly effective	above 50 % up to 75 %
3.	Effective	above 75 % up to 90 %
4.	very effective	above 90 %

1)   Vanti:

I F/U- Group A: cured patients were 20 & uncured were 23

Group B: cured patients were 15 & uncured were 26

Acco. to 'Chi Square test' results were 'Insignificant'.

II F/U- Group A: cured patients were 26 & uncured were 17

Group B: cured patients were 17 & uncured were 24

Acco. to 'Chi Square test' results were 'Insignificant'.

III F/U- Group A: cured patients were 32 & uncured were 11

Group B: cured patients were 21 & uncured were 20

Acco. to 'Chi Square test' results were 'Significant'.

IV F/U- Group A: cured patients were 38 & uncured were 05

Group B: cured patients were 32 & uncured were 09

Acco. to 'Chi Square test' results were 'Insignificant'.

Here, we can say that during first two follow-up progress was similar in both groups; but at third follow-up 'Nidan Parivarjan' played the key role in disease relief. Again in fourth follow-up it was insignificant. But this data is sufficient to prove importance of 'Nidan Parivarjan'

2)   Shiroruja:

I F/U- Group A: cured patients were 06 & uncured were 38

Group B: cured patients were 04 & uncured were 38

Acco. to 'Chi Square test' results were 'Insignificant'.

II F/U- Group A: cured patients were 10 & uncured were 34

Group B: cured patients were 05 & uncured were 37

Acco. to 'Chi Square test' results were 'Insignificant'.

III F/U- Group A: cured patients were 23 & uncured were 21

Group B: cured patients were 11 & uncured were 31

Acco. to 'Chi Square test' results were 'Significant'.

IV F/U- Group A: cured patients were 35 & uncured were 09

Group B: cured patients were 21 & uncured were 21

Acco. to 'Chi Square test' results were 'Significant'.

Here, during first two follow-up progress was similar in both groups; but in later stages Trial Group has shown excellent results confirming positive role of 'Nidan Parivarjan'.

3)   *Tikta-Amla Udgar:*

I F/U- Group A: cured patients were 08 & uncured were 38

Group B: cured patients were 06 & uncured were 39

Acco. to 'Chi Square test' results were 'Insignificant'.

II F/U- Group A: cured patients were 15 & uncured were 31

Group B: cured patients were 10 & uncured were 35

Acco. to 'Chi Square test' results were 'Insignificant'.

III F/U- Group A: cured patients were 27 & uncured were 19

Group B: cured patients were 16 & uncured were 29

Acco. to 'Chi Square test' results were 'Significant'.

IV F/U- Group A: cured patients were 36 & uncured were 10

Group B: cured patients were 23 & uncured were 22

Acco. to 'Chi Square test' results were 'Significant'.

In this symptom; results in both the group were non significant in first two follow-up. After that it is seen that trial group has better progress than control group.

4) *Hrid-Kantha Daha:*

I F/U- Group A: cured patients were 12 & uncured were 30

Group B: cured patients were 07 & uncured were 33

Acco. to 'Chi Square test' results were 'Insignificant'.

II F/U- Group A: cured patients were 20 & uncured were 22

Group B: cured patients were 11 & uncured were 29

Acco. to 'Chi Square test' results were 'Insignificant'.

III F/U- Group A: cured patients were 29 & uncured were 13

Group B: cured patients were 17 & uncured were 23

Acco. to 'Chi Square test' results were 'Significant'.

IV F/U- Group A: cured patients were 38 & uncured were 04

Group B: cured patients were 25 & uncured were 15

Acco. to 'Chi Square test' results were 'Significant'.

Here, during first two follow-up relief was similar in both groups; but in later stages Trial Group has shown excellent results confirming effective presence of *'Nidan Parivarjan'* in the treatment of the disease.

5) *Kara-Charan Daha:*

I F/U- Group A: cured patients were 11 & uncured were 18

Group B: cured patients were 06 & uncured were 20

Acco. to 'Chi Square test' results were 'Insignificant'.

II F/U- Group A: cured patients were 15 & uncured were 14

Group B: cured patients were 08 & uncured were 18

Acco. to 'Chi Square test' results were 'Insignificant'.

III F/U- Group A: cured patients were 22 & uncured were 07

Group B: cured patients were 10 & uncured were 16

Acco. to 'Chi Square test' results were 'Significant'.

IV F/U- Group A: cured patients were 25 & uncured were 04

Group B: cured patients were 12 & uncured were 14

Acco. to 'Chi Square test' results were 'Significant'.

In this symptom; results in both the group were non significant in first two follow-up. After that it is seen that trial group has better progress than control group. This proves that '*Nidan Parivarjan*' has major role in treatment.

6)   ***Sarvanga Daha:***

I F/U-   Group A: cured patients were 06 & uncured were 17

Group B: cured patients were 05 & uncured were 16

Acco. to 'Chi Square test' results were 'Insignificant'.

II F/U- Group A: cured patients were 13 & uncured were 10

Group B: cured patients were 07 & uncured were 14

Acco. to 'Chi Square test' results were 'Insignificant'.

III F/U- Group A: cured patients were 19 & uncured were 04

Group B: cured patients were 11 & uncured were 10

Acco. to 'Chi Square test' results were 'Significant'.

IV F/U- Group A: cured patients were 23 & uncured were 00

Group B: cured patients were 15 & uncured were 06

Acco. to 'Chi Square test' results were 'Significant'.

Here, during first two follow-up progress was similar in both groups; but in later stages Trial Group has shown excellent results confirming positive role of '*Nidan Parivarjan*'.

7)   ***Aruchi:***

I F/U-   Group A: cured patients were 09 & uncured were 11

Group B: cured patients were 05 & uncured were 13

Acco. to 'Chi Square test' results were 'Insignificant'.

II F/U- Group A: cured patients were 13 & uncured were 08

Group B: cured patients were 07 & uncured were 11

Acco. to 'Chi Square test' results were 'Insignificant'.

III F/U- Group A: cured patients were 17 & uncured were 04

Group B: cured patients were 09 & uncured were 09

Acco. to 'Chi Square test' results were '<u>Significant</u>'.

IV F/U- Group A: cured patients were 20 & uncured were 01

Group B: cured patients were 13 & uncured were 05

Acco. to 'Chi Square test' results were '<u>Significant</u>'.

In this symptom; results in both the group were similar, non significant in first two follow-up. After that it is seen that trial group has positive progress than control group. This proves that '*Nidan Parivarjan*' has played major role in relief.

8)   *Kandu:*

I F/U-   Group A: cured patients were 04 & uncured were 08

Group B: cured patients were 03 & uncured were 11

Acco. to 'Chi Square test' results were '<u>Insignificant</u>'.

II F/U- Group A: cured patients were 07 & uncured were 05

Group B: cured patients were 05 & uncured were 09

Acco. to 'Chi Square test' results were '<u>Insignificant</u>'.

III F/U- Group A: cured patients were 10 & uncured were 02

Group B: cured patients were 06 & uncured were 08

Acco. to 'Chi Square test' results were '<u>Significant</u>'.

IV F/U- Group A: cured patients were 12 & uncured were 00

Group B: cured patients were 11 & uncured were 03

Acco. to 'Chi Square test' results were '<u>Insignificant</u>'.

Here, we can say that during first two follow-up progress was similar in both groups; but at third follow-up '*Nidan Parivarjan*' played the key role in disease relief. Again in fourth follow-up it was insignificant. But this data is sufficient to prove importance of '*Nidan Parivarjan*'

9)   *Jvara:*

Number of patients having the symptom '*Jvara*' in both the groups is:

Group A: 03

Group B: 04

These numbers are very less; hence these are inadequate for statistical analysis by applying statistical tests like CHI^2 test.

That is why it is not practically possible to draw any inference from these numbers.

10)   *Mandal* & 11) *Pidaka* :

These two signs were totally absent in all patients from both the groups. Hence there is no chance of statistical analysis and inference.

<u>Overall relief in clinical features of *Urdhvag Amlapitta*:</u>

I F/U-   Group A: cured patients were 22 & uncured were 28

Group B: cured patients were 19 & uncured were 31

Acco. to 'Chi Square test' results were '<u>Insignificant</u>'.

II F/U- Group A: cured patients were 27 & uncured were 23

Group B: cured patients were 21 & uncured were 29

Acco. to 'Chi Square test' results were '<u>Insignificant</u>'.

III F/U- Group A: cured patients were 36 & uncured were 14

Group B: cured patients were 26 & uncured were 24

Acco. to 'Chi Square test' results were '<u>Significant</u>'.

IV F/U- Group A: cured patients were 42 & uncured were 08

Group B: cured patients were 33 & uncured were 17

Acco. to 'Chi Square test' results were '<u>Significant</u>'.

From above all observations it can be said that the effect of '*Nidan Parivarjan*' can not be seen in early stages like first 07 to 14 days of treatment. But, in later stages, after 28 to 30 days, if it is continued with patience & high degree of motivation, it will definitely give positive results & better, permanent relief and protection from the disease. This proves that *Nidan Parivarjan* has major role in *Samprapti Vighatan* and thus can be considered as '*Apunarbhav Chikitsa*'.

Retrospectively we can add that after *Nidan Parivarjan* symptomatic relief is achieved, means these all *Nidan/Hetu* must have definite role in *Samprapti* (disease formation). This proves all these '*Hetu*' described in our *Ayurvedic* texts.

7) <u>Summary:</u>

The present book entitled "*URDHVAG AMLAPITTA – HETU & NIDAN PARIVARJAN*" has been carried out to study the *Hetu* and their role in *Anshansh Samprapti* of the disease. We have observed the effects of *Nidan Parivarjan* on the signs & symptom of disease and from these effects; retrospectively we can confirm the role of *Nidan (Hetu)* in formation of the disease.

The study is disposed in following sections: Introduction, Aims & objectives, Review of literature, Material & Method, Observations & Results, Discussion and Conclusion.

1)   Aims & objectives:

In this topic; details regarding title of the book, need for selection and study of this topic, importance of *Nidan Parivarjan* etc. points are described.

2)   Review of literature:

In this chapter, Historical review of the disease is carried out from all possible ancient sources. *Ayurvedic* literature of *Amlapitta* is obtained from *Bruhat Trayi, Laghu Trayi* and other classics. Modern literature of the diseases co-related with *Amlapitta,* such as Hyperacidity, Gastric Ulcers etc. is collected from text books of Pathology & Medicine.

3)   Material and method:

Here in Material section; selection criteria for volunteers, sampling, Selection & preparation of the Drug etc. things are discussed.

In Methods; various phases like Diagnostic Phase, Interventional Phase, and Assessment Phase are explained in detail. Scoring & Grading for *Hetu Sevan* and Sign-Symptoms are given.

4)   Observations and Results:

Include the distribution of patients in different groups as per involvement of the disease, age, sex, *prakruti* etc. This part includes total score & statistical analysis of cured and uncured patients. Results obtained in both groups are displayed in the form of graphs and charts.

5)   Discussion:

In this chapter detail discussion is carried out with various aspects of the study regarding age, sex, *prakruti* of the patients; percentage of every *Hetu Sevan* grades in all 100 patients; step by step

Urdhvag Amlapitta - Hetu & Nidanparivarjan   Dr. Parag Kulkarni & Dr. Amar Abhrange

relief in clinical features of the disease in both groups and importance of '*Nidan Parivarjan*' from these results; role of *Hetu sevan* in *Anshansha Samprapti* of *Urdhvag Amlapitta;* co-relation of some modern life style *Hetu* with our classical *Ayurvedic Hetu.*

6)   Conclusion:

Includes end results of all the study which tends to fulfill all Aims & Objectives in various views and angles which states the total output of the study.

8) <u>Conclusion:</u>

This book entitled, "URDHVAG AMLAPITTA - HETU & NIDAN PARIVARJAN"- is aiming towards assessment of *Hetu Sevan* of *Urdhvag Amlapitta* by the patients and assessment of effects of *Nidan Parivarjan* on the signs-symptoms.

Here are some highlighting facts revealed in the study regarding this topic:

1) *Urdhvag Amlapitta* is such a leading problem in today's life that large numbers of patients visiting to OPDs were complaining about this disease; among those eligible volunteers were taken in to consideration for the study.

2) Number of Male patients was comparatively more than the Females.

3) Patients in the age group in between 31 yrs to 40 yrs were more affected by the disease.

4) Prevalence of the disease was more in *Pitta-Kapha Prakruti* indivisuals.

5) If occupation is concerned, Servicemen or Working Class people were slightly more involved than others.

6) As far as *Hetu Sevan* is concerned; various *Hetu* were observed in various concentrations in the disease *Samprapti.* Among those few examples are as follows:

➢ *Hetu* like *Adhyashan, pishtanna, Atyushna, Ratrijagaran* were observed in the study; they were consumed in *"Alpasevan"* concentration.

➢ *Hetu* like *Atisnigdha, Atidrava, Pruthuk, Antarodaka* were more observed in *"Madhyamsevan"* concentration.

➢ *Hetu* like Guru-Abhishyandi, Fanit-Ikshu vikar were more observed in *"Atisevan"* concentration.

7) Some new *Hetu* were found other than *Ayurvedic* texts like *Ratrijagaran,* Addictions, Medicinal intake and those can be co-related with respective category of *Ayurvedic Hetu.*

8) Probable role of *Hetu Sevan* in the *Anshansh Samprapti* of the disease can be satisfactorily explained on the basis of signs & symptoms observed.

9) Descending order of specific clinical features of the disease on the basis of Number of patients observed is- *Vanti, Shiroruja, Tikta Amla Udgar, Hrid-Kantha Daha, Kara-Charan daha, Sarvang Daha, Aruchi, Kandu, Jvara.*

10) Positive effects of *Nidan Parivarjan* were clearly observed in the interventional phase of the study. Both groups 'A' & 'B' were going on the same lines in first Two follow-up in about all sign-symptoms. But in Third & Fourth follow-up the 'Trial group A' showed significant progress in disease relief.

11) *Nidan Parivarjan* will not give significant results in early stages but it is very effective if practiced with patience & high degree of motivation for a long time. This relief will be permanent & long lasting.

12) *Nidan Parivarjan* reduces sign-symptoms; retrospectively we can confirm all those *Nidanas (Hetu)* described in our *Ayurvedic* classics.

13) Thus, the concept like *Nidan Parivarjan*, once again establishes the image of *Ayurved* as 'Curative' as well as a 'Preventive Medicine'.

।। स्वस्थस्य स्वास्थ्यरक्षणं आतुरस्य व्याधिपरिमोक्षः ।।

9) Abbreviations:

C. Su.	Charak Sutrasthan
C. Ni.	Charak Nidansthan
C. Ch.	*Charak Chikitsasthan*
C. Sha.	*Charak Sharirasthan*
C. Vi.	*Charak Vimansthan*
C. Si.	*Charak Sidhisthan*
S. Su.	*Sushrut Sutrasthan*
S. Sh.	*Sushrut Sharirsthan*
S. Ch.	*Sushrut Chikitsasthan*
A.H. Su.	*Ashtang Hriday Sutrasthan*
A.H.U.	*Ashtang Hriday Uttar Tantra*
M. N.	*Madhav Nidan*
SH. S.	*Sharangadhar Samhita*
A.H. Ni.	*Ashtang Hriday Nidansthan*
A.H. Ch.	*Ashtang Hriday Chikitsasthan*
A.H. Sh.	*Ashtang Hriday Sharirsthan*
A. S. Su.	*Ashtang Sangrah Sutrasthan*
A.S. Ni.	*Ashtang Sangrah Nidansthan*
CH	*Charak Samhita*
SU	*Sushrut Samhita*
A. S.	*Ashtag Sangraha*
K. S.	*Kashyap Samhita*
R.R.S	*Rasa-ratna Samuchchay*
Y. R.	*Yog Ratnakar*
B. P.	*Bhav Prakash*
H. S.	*Harit Samhita*
G. N.	*Gadnigraha*
CHK	*Chakradatta*
S. N.	Serial Number
x^2	Chi Square
L of S	Level of Significance
D.F. 1	Degree of Freedom
FU	Follow Up
No.	Number
Yrs.	Years
%	Percentage

10) References:

1. *Vedon main Ayurved*: Dr. Kapil Dev Dwivedi, Vishwa Bharati Anusandhan Parishd, Varanasi, 1993.
2. *The Shabdakalpadrum*: Raja Radha Kant Dev, Nag publishers, Delhi, 1987.
3. *Cahrak Samhita*: Kashinath Shashtri, Gorakh Nath Chaturvedi, Choukhambha Bharati Academy, Varanasi, 1998.
4. *Charak Samhita with Chakrapani Teeka*: Vaidya Yadav Sharma, Rashtriya Sanskrit Sansthan, Delhi, 2006.
5. *Charak Samhita*: Dr. Ramcharan Sharma and Vaidya Bhagawan Das, Choukhambha Sansktut Series, Varanasi, 1976.
6. *Sushrut Samhita*: Ambikadatta Shashtri, 12th edition, Choukhambha Sanskrut Pratishthan, Varanasi, 2001.
7. *Sushrut Samhita*: K. L. Bhishagratna, 5th edition, Choukhambha Sansktut Series, Varanasi, 1976.
8. *Sushrut Samhita*: Acharya Yadavji Trikamji, 4th edition, Choukhambha Orientalis, Varanasi, 1980.
9. *Astang Hridayam*: Dr. Bramhanand Tripathi, Choukhambha Sanskrut Pratishthan, Varanasi, 2003.
10. *Astang Hridayam*: Anna Moreshwar Kunte, Choukhambha Sanskrut Pratishthan, Varanasi, 2002.
11. *Astang Sangrah*: Lal Chandra Shastri, 1st edition, Shri Baidyanath Ayurved Bhavan Limited, Nagpur, 1959.
12. *Chakradatta*: Indradeva Tripathi, 4th edition, choukhambha Sanskrit Pratisthan, Varanasi, 2002.
13. *Madhav Nidanam*: Vaidya Sudarshan Shastri, 28th edition, choukhambha Sanskrit Pratisthan, Varanasi, 1999.
14. *Madhav Nidanam*: Prof. K. R. Shrikanta Murthy, Choukhambha Orientalis, Varanasi, 1987.
15. *Bhavaprakash Nighantu*: Dr. K. C. Chunekar, Choukhambha Bharati Academy, Varanasi, 2002.
16. *Sharangdhar Samhita*: K. R. Shrikant Murthy, 3rd edition, Choukhambha Orientalis, Varanasi, 1997.
17. *Yogaratnakar*: Nirmal Saxena, 1st edition, Choukhambha Orientalis, Varanasi, 1995.
18. *Kashyap Samhita of vridha jivaka tantra, vidyadini tika,*- Pandit hemraj sharma, 8th edition, Choukhamba Sanskrit snasthan varanasi, 2001.
19. *Siddhant Nidanam*: Gananath Sen, 5th edition, Choukhambha Sanskrit Series, Varanasi, 1966.
20. *Sharangdhar Samhita*: Brhmhanand Tripathi, choukhambha Sanskrit Pratisthan, Varanasi, 2004.
21. *Rogi Rog Pariksha Padhati*: Dr. G. P. Upadhyay, Choukhambha Sanskrit Series, Varanasi, 1997.
22. Differential Diagnosis: Dr. G. P. Upadhyay, Arpit Prakashan, Nagpur, 2002.
23. *Kaya Chikitsa*: Dr. Ram Harsha Singh, Choukhambha Sanskrit Pratishthan, Varanasi, 2004.
24. *Kaya Chikitsa*: Dr. Vidyadhar Shukla, 4th edition, Choukhambha Subharati Prakashan, Varanasi, 1999.
25. *Abhinav Kaya Chikitsa*: Anant Ram Sharma, choukhambha Sanskrit Pratisthan, Varanasi, 2002.
26. *Ayurvediya Vikruti Vidnyan*: Dr Vidyadhar Shukla, 5th edition, Choukhambha Sanskrit Pratisthan, Varanasi, 1999.
27. *Nidan Chikitsa Hastamalak*: Dr. Ranjeet Rai Desai, 2nd edition, Shri Baidyanath Ayurved Bhavan Limited, Nagpur, 1990.
28. *Ayurvediya Shabda Kosha*: Veni Madhav Shastri Joshi, Narayan Hari Joshi, Maharashtra Rajya Sahitya and Sanskriti Mandal, Mumbai, 1968.

29. *Ayurvediya Kriya Sharir*: Dr. Ranjeet Rai Desai, Shri Baidyanath Ayurved Bhavan Limited, Nagpur, 1990.

30. *Ayurved Ka Vaigyanik Itihas*: Prof. P. V. Sharma, 2nd edition, Choukhambha Orientalis, Varanasi, 1981.

31. Harrison's Principles of Internal Medicine: 15th edition, Mc Grew Hill Company, Columbus, 2001.

32. Davidson's Principles and Practice of Medicine: 18th edition, Harcourt Publishers Limited, U. K., 1999.

33. Human Physiology: C. C. Chattergee, 11th edition, Medical Allied Agency, Calcutta, 1994.

34. API Text Book of Medicine: G. C. Sainani, 6th edition, Associations of Physicians of India, 2001.

35. Understanding Human Anatomy & Physiology, Fifth Edition, © The McGraw −Hill Companies.

36. Text book of Pathology: Harsha Mohan, 3rd edition, Jaypee Brothers Medical Publishers (P) Limited, Noida, 1998.

37. Methods in Biostatistics: B. K. Mahajan, 16th edition, Jaypee Brothers Medical Publishers (P) Limited, Noida, 2004.

38. Websites- www.wikipedia.com
    www.medindia.net
    www.healthyfellow.com
    www.rch.org.au
    www.pacificwellness.ca
    www.healthinplainenglish.com
    www.medical-look.com